Human Image:
World Image

Human Image: World Image

THE DEATH AND RESURRECTION OF SACRED COSMOLOGY

Philip Sherrard

DENISE HARVEY (PUBLISHER)

LIMNI, EVIA, GREECE

First published by Golgonooza Press, 1992,
with the financial assistance of
Friends of the Centre

Reprinted in 2004 by
Denise Harvey (Publisher), 340 05 Limni, Evia, Greece

Copyright © Denise Harvey (Publisher)
Printed in Greece

ISBN 960-7120-17-5

Contents

Author's Acknowledgement and Dedication

As is inevitably the case with a book of this kind, none of the main ideas guiding its argument and determining its conclusions is my own invention, in the sense that I have originated it. For virtually every statement I am dependent on what I have learnt from others. Some of those to whom I am indebted are indicated in the text, but others are not specified. Between them they include St Justin Martyr, St Irenaeus, St Clement of Alexandria, Origen, the author of the *Corpus Dionysiacum*, Syriac authors such as St Ephrem and St Isaac of Nineveh, St Maximos the Confessor, John Scottus Eriugena, St Simeon the New Theologian, Meister Eckhart, Jan Van Ruysbroeck, Plotinus, Proklos, Jacob Boehme, William Blake, W. B. Yeats, Vladimir Solovieff, P. A. Florensky, G. Florovsky, Alexis van den Mensbrugghe, Rumi, Titus Burckhardt, Henry Corbin, Marco Pallis, the authors of the Upanishads, Ananda K. Coomaraswamy, Sisirkumar Ghose, Kapila Vatsyayan, Sunderlal Bahnguna, Chief Seattle, Black Elk, Wendell Berry, Rabbi Schneur Zalman, Gershom G. Scholem, R. G. Collingwood, C. S. Lewis, and many others. I am beholden to all of them, and to all I dedicate this book, and can only apologize if I have placed all or any of them in a context or among company with which they would have preferred not to have been associated.

Philip Sherrard
Katounia
Limni
Winter 1991

Introduction

ONE THING at least we no longer need to be told is that we are in the throes of a crisis of the most appalling dimensions. We tend to call this crisis the ecological crisis, and this is a fair description in so far as its effects are manifest above all in the ecological sphere. For here the message is quite clear: our entire way of life is humanly and environmentally suicidal, and unless we change it radically there is no way in which we can avoid cosmic catastrophe. Without such change the whole adventure of civilization will come to an end during the lifetime of many now living.

Unhappily we do not yet appear to have realized the urgency of the need for such a change, and in spite of everything we continue to blunder on along our present path of devastation in a kind of blindfold nightmare enacted with all the inevitability of a Greek tragedy, planning to extend our empire of sterilized artificiality and specialist methodology even further, advancing even further into the computerized or electronic wilderness, devising bigger and better banking systems, manipulating the natural reproductive processes of plants, animals and human beings, saturating our soils and crops with high-powered chemicals and a variety of poisons which no sane community would allow out of a closely-guarded laboratory, stripping the world of what is left of its forests at a speed which defies belief or understanding, and behaving generally in a manner which, even if we had deliberately programmed it, could not be more propitious to our own annihilation and to that of the world about us. It is as if we are in the grip of some monstrous collective psychosis, as if in truth a huge death-wish hangs over the whole so-called civilized world.

In the ecological sphere the message is, as I said, unambiguously clear, however much we may continue to ignore it. Yet although the effects of our contemporary crisis are most evident in this sphere, the crisis itself is not first of all an ecological crisis. It is not first of all a crisis concerning our environment. It is first of all a crisis concerning the way we think. We are treating our planet in an inhuman, god-forsaken manner because we see things in an inhuman, god-forsaken way. And we see things in this way because that basically is how we see ourselves.

This is the first thing about which we have to be absolutely clear if we are even to begin to find a way out of the hells of self-mutilation to which we have condemned ourselves. How we see the world depends above all upon how we see ourselves. Our model of the universe—our world-picture or world image—is based upon the model we have of ourselves, upon our own self-image. When we look at the world, what we see is a reflection of our own mind, of our own mode of consciousness. Our perception of a tree, a mountain, a face, an animal or a bird is a reflection of our idea of who we think we are. What we experience in these things is not so much the reality or nature of these things in themselves as simply that which our own limitations, spiritual, psychological and physical, permit us to experience of them. Our capacity to perceive and experience is stereotyped according to how we have moulded our own image and likeness.

This means that before we can effectively deal with the ecological problem we have to change our world image, and this in its turn means that we have to change our self-image. Unless our own evaluation of ourselves, and of what constitutes the true nature of our being, changes, the way we treat the world about us will not change either. And unless that happens, conservation theory and practice, however well-intentioned and necessary, will not touch the heart of the problem. They will at best represent an effort to deal with what in the end are symptoms, not causes.

I do not in the least want to belittle such efforts, which often are heroic, lonely and incredible, against all odds. One of the terrible temptations we face is that of thinking that the problem is so big that nothing we can do on an individual scale can possibly have any effect: we must leave it to the authorities, to the governments, to the experts.

That is a fatal attitude. Every single gesture made, however pathetic it may seem, counts, and may have incalculable consequences. Thought not accompanied by corresponding practice soon becomes sterile. Yet at the same time practice springing from incorrectly based thought easily becomes counter-productive, because practice deals above all with symptoms. Causes are rooted in the way we think, and it is because of this that our crisis is first of all a question of our self-image and our world-view.

This is the crux of our situation. The industrial and technological inferno we have produced around us, and by means of which we are now devastating our world, is not something that has come about accidentally. On the contrary, it is the direct consequence of our allowing ourselves to be dominated by a certain paradigm of thought—embracing a certain human image and a certain world image—to such a degree that it now determines virtually all our mental attitudes and all our actions, public and private.

It is a paradigm of thought that impels us to look upon ourselves as little more than two-legged animals whose destiny and needs can best be fulfilled through the pursuit of social, political and economic self-interest. And to correspond with this self-image we have invented a world-view in which nature is seen as an impersonal commodity, a soulless source of food, raw materials, wealth, power and so on, which we think we are quite entitled to experiment with, exploit, remodel and generally abuse by means of any scientific and mechanical technique we can devise and produce, in order to satisfy and deploy this self-interest. Having in our own minds desanctified ourselves, we have desanctified nature, too, in our own minds: we have removed it from the suzerainty of the divine and have assumed that we are its overlords, and that it is our thrall, subject to our will. In short, under the aegis of this self-image and world-view we have succeeded in converting ourselves into the most depraved and depraving of all creatures upon the earth.

This self-image and world-view have their origin in a loss of memory, in a forgetfulness of who we are, and in our fall to a level of ignorance and stupidity that threatens the survival of our race. By an inescapable logic inherent in this origin we are impelled to proceed along a course each step of which is marked by our fall into ever deeper ignorance of our own nature and consequently into ever deeper ignorance of the nature of everything else as well.

So long as we persist in this course, we are doomed to advance blindly and at an ever-increasing pace towards total loss of identity, total loss of control and eventually to total self-destruction. And nothing can stop this process except a complete reversal of direction, a complete change in the way we look at ourselves and so in the way we look at the world about us. Without that change, we will simply continue to add fuel to our own funeral pyre.

Can we make this reversal, this complete change? I think the answer to that is that no one can stop us doing so except ourselves. No one can stop us from changing our own self-image and consequently our world-view except ourselves.

The question—the only real question—is what self-image and world-view are we to put in the place of the bankrupt stereotypes, the unensouled fictions, which have taken us over?

Here a certain act of recollection is needed. I said that the self-image and world-view that now dominate us have their origin in a loss of memory, in our forgetfulness of who we are. What do I mean by this?

In the great creative cultures of the world, human beings do not regard themselves as two-legged animals, descended from the apes, whose needs and satisfactions can be achieved through pursuing social, political and economic self-interest in the material world and as though their life was confined to a material space-time dimension. On the contrary, they think of themselves first and foremost as descended from the gods, or from God, and as heirs to eternity, with a destiny that goes far beyond politics, society and economics, or anything that can be fulfilled in terms of the material world or by satisfying their mortal and physical desires and needs. They think of themselves as sacred beings, even as semi-divine beings, not in their own right, but because they are created in the divine image, in the image of God, of a transcendent more-than-human form of consciousness. They come from a divine source, and the divine world is their birthright, their true home.

In the same way, they do not look upon what we call the outer world, the world of nature, as a mere chance association of atoms or whatever, or as something impersonal, soulless, inanimate, which they are entitled to manipulate, master, exploit and generally to tamper and mess about with in order to gratify their greeds and their power-lusts. They look upon nature, too, as a divine creation, as full of a hidden wisdom as they themselves are, as full of a personal, sensitive soul-life or psychic life as they themselves are. They recognize and acknowledge in nature, too, a sacred reality, a divine invisible presence made visible. They sense that every part of the earth—of the whole cosmos—is sacred. Every leaf, every grain of sand or soil, every bird, animal and star, the air and every insect is holy, instinct with life, in their memory and experience. The sap which courses through the trees is as sacred as their own life-blood—is one with their own life-blood. Forests, mountains, lakes, fields, seas, the great plains and even the deserts are not 'resources' for exploitation; they are a way of life. They may trade in the gifts they offer—in precious stones and spices, in corn and cattle. They may in ignorance be excessive in their demands on them, in grazing their flocks or in felling too many trees. But they do not deliberately *trade in nature itself*, or at the expense of nature. They do not, and could not (*not* simply because they lack the technical know-how) deliberately blast its guts out through testing their atom and nuclear bombs, savage its skies with the din and stench of aeroplanes and space-craft, poison its rivers, its lakes, its seas, its underground waters through spilling chemicals into them or through the leaching of toxic wastes, or rape it in any of the thousands of ways in which we are now raping it.

And when I say 'could not', I do not mean this in any sentimental sense. It is an interdiction rooted in the profoundest depths of their understanding of things. If nature is the creation of God, or the manifestation of Supreme Wisdom and Harmony, it follows not only that it is the expression of a divine order and disposition, but also that this order and disposition are the best that are possible, given the conditions under which or within which nature is created or made manifest. Consequently, for us to imagine that we can improve it, or remove the imperfections inherent in it, by interfering with it, re-modelling it, transforming it and so on, through ways that involve disrupting or perverting its God-given order and disposition as well as the organic processes that are part and parcel of them, is sheer folly and impertinence: it is to imagine that we can outstrip and improve on the wisdom of Wisdom Absolute. Inevitably, therefore, any attempt on our part so to interfere in it or to re-model it can only debase, canker, corrupt and vitiate the conditions in which we have to live our life on earth. Over the last few centuries we have so effectively demonstrated the truth of this that we should not need any further convincing as to the rightness of the understanding in which it is rooted.

Yet, in spite of this, such an understanding, and the sense of the sacredness of both man and nature, as well as the awe and reverence that they inspire, are often characterized nowadays as primitive, or as based on superstition, and regarded as belonging to the pre-scientific age and as something promoted only by those who have failed, for whatever reason, to move into the twentieth century (or the twenty-first century, as it soon will be). To maintain that theories of biological evolution, whether in a Darwinian or post-Darwinian form, are misconceived, and that human beings, far from being descended from the apes, only develop ape-like propensities and features when they pervert their human nature and become sub-human, or anti-human, is still to invite ridicule. To insist that we can obtain no genuine knowledge of the physical world unless we first attain a knowledge of spiritual or metaphysical realities is to provoke the accusation of obscurantism, if not plain dottiness: we tend to take it for granted that not only is it perfectly possible to obtain a knowledge of the physical world without any reference whatsoever to the idea of a God, or a Creator, or of any underlying trans-temporal and trans-spatial metaphysical reality, but also that we positively must *not* allow any such idea to determine either the methods we employ in our search for knowledge or the substance of what we put forward as knowledge. We can and must examine visible nature (*natura naturata*) as though it were independent of the invisible metaphysical nature (*natura naturans*) from which it derives and in which it is rooted. We can and must explain natural phenomena as though they were independent of the realm of the supranatural. We can and must explain them merely in terms of the laws of physics and chemistry, without any reference to *natura naturans* or to the realm of the supranatural. Such is the level to which the human intelligence has degenerated in its pursuit of the goals that typify our modern world.

And this in spite of the fact that—to limit ourselves to the European tradition alone—there is no major philosopher, from Plato to Berdyaev, and no major poet, from Homer to Yeats, who has not explicitly or implicitly affirmed the kind of cosmology that we now tend to ridicule, repudiate or ignore. One of the great unresolved psychological enigmas of the modern western world is the question of what or who has persuaded us to accept as virtually axiomatic a self-view and a world-view that demand that we reject out of hand the wisdom and vision of our major philosophers and poets in order to imprison our thought and our very selves in the materialist, mechanical and dogmatic torture-chamber devised by purely quantitative and third-rate scientific minds.

In this connection there is one particular fallacy from which we must free ourselves, and this is the idea that contemporary scientific theories, and the descriptions that go with them, are somehow neutral, or value-free, and do not presuppose the submission of the human mind to a set of assumptions or dogmas in the way that is said to be demanded by

6

adherence to a religious faith. This idea is, indeed, still propagated and even believed by many modern scientists themselves. On it is based the claim that scientific descriptions of things are objective descriptions. It is not that these scientists deny that there are, or may be, values. It is that in so far as they are scientists they claim to operate independently of value-judgments, and to be engaged in what they like to call purely disinterested scientific research.

This is one of the most insidious of the fallacies of which we still tend to be the victims. Even people who maintain that they are fighting for a new philosophy of ecological values, such as Henryk Skolimowski,[1] repeat it as though it were beyond dispute. In fact, far from being beyond dispute, it represents a total lie. Every thought, every observation, every judgment, every description whether of the modern scientist or of anyone else is soaked in *a priori* preconceived built-in value-judgments, assumptions and dogmas at least as rigid, if not more rigid (because they are so often unconsciously embraced) than those of any explicitly religious system. The very nature of human thought is such that it cannot operate independently of value-judgments, assumptions and dogmas. Even the assertion that it can constitutes a value-judgment and implies a whole philosophy, whether we are aware of it or not.

Alongside this fallacy, and closely allied to it, is another fallacy of which we still tend to be the victims. This is the notion—already alluded to—not that modern science is value-free, or that it is the only possible science, but that it is valid in relation to that limited aspect of things —namely, that aspect of them which is material or phenomenal, and extended in time and space—that it sets out to study. This notion is not intended to deny that there is, or may be, another aspect of things—that which is spiritual and eternal, and unextended in time and space—that can also be studied in its own right and could be said to constitute the sphere of spiritual knowledge or of a spiritual science. It simply involves the claim that there are two levels of reality; that each level can be studied apart from, and without reference to, the other; and that the knowledge gained as a result of studying the one level is just as valid in its own terms as the knowledge gained as a result of studying the other level.

This way of envisaging things is a fallacy because the primary determinant of the knowledge—or what we assume to be the knowledge

---

1. See his article, 'World-views and values for the future', in *India International Centre Quarterly*, Spring 1989, p.159.

—that we form of things is not the particular level of reality to which this knowledge is said to apply. Its primary determinant is the level or mode of consciousness of which this knowledge is the expression. This is to say that it is not so much that there are different levels of reality to perceive and experience, the one inner and spiritual and the other outer and material, each with an independent science that corresponds to it. It is that there are different levels or modes of consciousness in man through which he perceives and experiences; so that what he perceives and experiences will depend first of all on the level or mode of consciousness active within him, and not on the level of reality that he happens to be studying.

There are not two sciences, the one concerned with the material and outward aspect of things extended in time and space, and the other with their spiritual and eternal dimension, unextended in time and space. There is only one science. But there are two dominant modes of consciousness in man: his ego-consciousness, which is his lowest mode of consciousness, corresponding as it does to what is most inhuman and satanic in him; and his angelic or spiritual consciousness, which is his higher mode of consciousness. Of course, there are endless permutations between these two modes, depending on whether the consciousness gravitates more to the one or to the other.

The higher or spiritual consciousness perceives and experiences things as they are in themselves, inner and outer, spiritual and material, metaphysical and physical interpenetrating and forming a single unsundered and unsunderable reality. The profane or ego-consciousness cannot perceive and experience things as they are. It can perceive and experience only what its own opacity permits it to perceive and experience, and that is not the reality of things but things emasculated of their reality. There cannot be a science of things—of phenomena—which ignores the reality of phenomena, that by virtue of which they are what they are. There cannot be a valid science of the physical aspect of things alone, for the simple reason that the notion that things possess an outer physical aspect apart from their inner spiritual dimension is an illusory notion.

For if we could perceive and experience with the full clarity of our higher or spiritual consciousness, we would be able to see and understand that no visible thing—nothing belonging to the world of phenomena—possesses existence or being in its own right. We would see and understand that apart from its inner and spiritual dimension and identity it possesses no reality whatsoever, whether physical, material or substan-

8

tial, and that the notion that it does so is merely an illusion or distortion inherent as such in the viewpoint of the ego-consciousness. In no way is it possible to separate physics from metaphysics, and in so far as we think it is possible we simply confirm the inanity of our thought.

Thus in so far as modern science presupposes the notion that we can obtain a knowledge of phenomena apart from, and without reference to, a prior knowledge of their inner and spiritual dimension, it is based totally upon the ego-consciousness, or—which comes to the same thing—it is still in servitude to a dualism that opposes mind and matter, subject and object, the knower and what is to be known—a dualism which represents a total distortion of reality. This means it is tainted with the inhuman and satanic characteristics in man of which this consciousness is the vehicle. That it why its application, in technological or other forms, is liable to be fraught with consequences that are equally inhuman and satanic, whether with regard to our own being or with regard to the natural physical world.

That, too, is why every extension of the empire and influence of our contemporary secular scientific mentality has gone and continues to go hand in hand with a corresponding and increased erosion in us of the sense of the sacred. In fact, we do not have any respect, let alone reverence, for the world of nature because we do not fundamentally have any respect, let alone reverence for ourselves. It is because we have lost the sense of our own reality that we have lost the sense of every other reality as well. It is because we cripple and mutilate ourselves that we cripple and mutilate everything else as well. Our contemporary crisis is really our own depravity writ large.

So the only real answer to this crisis is to stop depraving ourselves. It is to recover a sense of our true identity and dignity, of our self-image as sacred beings, as immortal beings. A false self-view breeds a false world-view, and together they breed our nemesis and the nemesis of the world. Once we repossess a sense of our own holiness, we will recover the sense of the holiness of the world about us as well, and we will then act towards the world about us with the awe and humility that we should possess when we enter a sacred shrine, a temple of love and beauty in which we worship and adore. Only in this way will we once again become aware that our destiny and the destiny of nature are one and the same. Only in this way can we restore a cosmic harmony. If we do not take this way out, then that is that, for there is no other way out. To fail here is to fail irrevocably: there can be no escaping our inhuman genocide.

Without a sense of the holy—that everything that lives is holy—and without humility towards the whole—towards man, nature and *towards that which is beyond both man and nature*, their transcendent source and origin—we will simply proceed headlong along the course to self-destruction to which we are now committed, to that nemesis which is our own choosing and for which we are entirely responsible.

All this means that if we are to confront our contemporary crisis in a way that goes to its roots our task is twofold. We have first to get absolutely clear in our minds—to identify coherently and unquestion-ably—the paradigm of thought that underlies and determines our present self-image and world-view. Unless we first do this we are liable to become victims of a kind of double-think, attacking the symptoms while remaining subject to the causes that produce the symptoms. And it is all the more important for us to do it because we have tended to forget what the assumptions and presuppositions that characterize this paradigm are: they are so deeply embedded beneath the ramparts of our ordinary thought-processes that we are unaware that they do in fact underlie and determine these processes.

Second, we have to try to recover, or rediscover, the vision of man and nature—or, rather, the theoanthropocosmic vision—that will make it possible for us to perceive and hence to experience both ourselves and the world we live in as the sacred realities that they are; because unless we do recover a sense of their sacredness that is based upon a coherent under-standing of why they are sacred, our attempts to re-affirm this quality in them may be debilitated by what in the end is little more than senti-mental prejudice.

Our enquiry, therefore, is simultaneously anthropological—con-cerned with the question of who man is—and cosmological—concerned with the question of the nature of the universe. It is ultimately an attempt to re-affirm sacred images of both man and nature: to affirm a sacred human image and a sacred world image.

1 Forms of Sacred Cosmology in the Pre-Renaissance World

THE INITIAL thesis of this book is that in the centuries subsequent to the Renaissance we have increasingly lost our sense of living in a sacred universe, and that this has had disastrous consequences in every sphere of our lives. But in order to clarify how this loss of consciousness has come about, and to perceive what it amounts to, we have to set it within the perspective of the sacred cosmologies—and to a certain extent anthropologies—of the mediaeval Christian and pre-Christian, Greek and Roman, worlds; for only in this way can the loss in question become intelligible and its full significance be grasped. This is all the more the case because the desecration of cosmology in the post-Renaissance period was initiated by a revolt against the Christian understanding of things, and this revolt is characterized by a tendency, however erratic, to find in the pre-Christian world models for what was to become the new secular cosmic and human image.

This task of describing the sacred cosmologies of the pre-Renaissance world may well begin with Plato, for he is a key figure not only where the cosmology of the ancient Greek world is concerned, but also for mediaeval Christian and even for post-Renaissance, secular scientific cosmology. Yet if Plato is a key figure, he is not altogether a straightforward one. His philosophy in this respect is complex and even contradictory. For our purpose it is enough to indicate but two of what appear to be its contradictory aspects. On the one hand, there is Plato the dualist, whose dualism appears to be of an extreme nature. Aristotle called Plato a Pythagorean, and this is a true description at least to the extent that Plato

11

inherited from the Pythagoreans the idea that the reality of things in the physical or natural world—that by virtue of which they are what they are—is geometrical structure or form.[1] Once this idea is accepted, certain consequences follow, of which perhaps the most important is that by basing physics in this way on the principle of mathematics, you posit the presuppositions not only that the essence of natural objects is supremely intelligible but also that their supreme intelligibility can be expressed in mathematical terms.

Of course, this can be the case only provided the essence of natural objects, and not merely the shape or pattern they may assume, is in fact constituted by their geometrical structure or form: and it was precisely such an assumption that the Pythagoreans accepted as axiomatic. For them, it is the form in such objects that makes them behave as they do behave, that makes them what they are and constitutes their intrinsic nature; and this form, being mathematical, is intelligible. And a plurality of such forms constitutes what may be called a world of intelligibles, or an intelligible world, as distinct from the world of sensible or sensory realities, the physical world.

However it may have been for the Pythagoreans, in one aspect of Plato's thought emphasis on the transcendence of the intelligible world of pure forms is pushed so far that to all intents and purposes the physical world appears to be stripped of all reality whatsoever. Only the intelligible is real, and the intelligible is not physical at all. Physicality is one characteristic of things accessible to sense-perception, and what is accessible to sense-perception is not intelligible. Intelligibility is the privilege of mathematical forms alone, and hence only these forms can be said to possess reality, and they in their nature totally transcend the world of things accessible to sense-perception. In this side of Plato's thought, exemplified in such dialogues as the *Symposium*, *Phaedo* and the *Republic*, there appears to be a complete gulf between the world accessible to the senses—the world of nature—which is ultimately negative in character, and the transcendent world of pure forms, in which alone reality is to be found.

There is, however, another aspect of Plato's thought which from the point of view of subsequent developments is perhaps of more importance. According to this aspect the dualism of which we have spoken is, if

1. Here and elsewhere when discussing Platonic and Aristotelian cosmology, I am indebted to R. G. Collingwood's *The Idea of Nature* (Oxford, 1945), Part I, pp. 29–92.

not eliminated, at least attenuated, and the transcendence theory is counter-balanced by a theory in which the world of forms is seen as immanent in the physical world. For the physical world—the world of nature as it appears to us through the senses—possesses certain formal elements, and in so far as it does possess them it may be said to be intelligible. It is intelligible because by virtue of its formal elements it participates in or imitates the intelligible world of pure form. This implies a theory in which the intelligible world is neither transcendent to visible things nor entirely immanent in them. To some extent—to the extent that it possesses geometric structure or form—the physical world is in its own right intelligible; and to this extent it is a real world.

This second aspect of Plato's thought, in which the attempt is made to express the immanence of reality—the interrelationship of the visible and the invisible, the sensory and the intelligible—is most evident in his later dialogues. At the time when he wrote the *Republic*, he attributed no positive significance to the sensible world because this world, being in disorder (*en ataxia*), was without value. But in his later dialogues, in above all the *Timaeus* and the *Laws*, as the question of actually realizing the ideal city on earth became for him more and more pressing, so he was increasingly compelled to grope for a vision which would embrace the sensible world—this disorder—and would integrate it with the intelligible world, with the total divine order of the cosmos. He was compelled to face the problem of reconciling the immutable world of pure form with the changing world of the senses, and of finding some positive relationship between the one and the other. He had to escape from the dualism of Being and Becoming, intelligible and sensible, by which he had hitherto been dominated, and to approach more closely the dynamic vision of a Herakleitos, who found in movement itself the secret of stability.

The solution for which he sought is first indicated in the *Phaedrus*,[2] where the Soul is said to be the origin of movement (*arche tis kineseos*), and not something static as it had previously been regarded. This new approach is developed in the *Timaeus*. The Soul, the origin of movement, is self-moving, yet moves after the pattern of the immutable intelligible world. It is an intermediary between the eternal world of forms and the sensible world. Human morality must be founded on the order of the cosmos. The human soul is linked to the Soul of the World. There is in the *Timaeus* a sort of trinity of Intellect, Soul (from which comes life and

2. *Phaedrus*, 245 D.

movement) and Body of the World. There is what one might call a process of incarnation, embryonic as yet but capable of great development. The changing sensible world takes its place in the world of Being: it is rooted in the divine world. The trinity of Intellect, Soul and Body forms 'the sum total of Being' (the *pantelos on* of the *Sophist*).[3] The world is eternal, a divine Cosmos, an order always in movement that is subordinate to the Soul of the World, that is also eternal. The world is a living organism, the living body of the divine, and its revelation. Plato is here approaching a vision of the reciprocity between the sensible and the intelligible that is far more muted in his earlier dialogues.

No doubt the gulf between the world of the senses and the world of intelligible forms is never completely bridged in Plato's thought. A residual dualism is always present. Form, in which alone full reality resides, is in an absolute sense always transcendent, never immanent. Particular visible things cannot achieve pure form; they cannot be instances or total embodiments of pure form. The formal elements they possess—those that give them a degree of intelligibility and hence of reality—constitute their essence, that which makes them what they are. But these formal elements are not to be identified with pure form itself. They are only approximations to this form. The immanent form is not the transcendent form; it is but its 'imitation'.

As for those elements in visible things that are impervious to form and formal coherence, they are by definition unintelligible and hence unreal. Such elements tend to be identified with matter. Neoplatonists were later to attribute to the recalcitrance of matter the failure of natural forms to embody pure form, and thus they saw matter as the cause of imperfection and even of evil itself; and such a conclusion may be said to be latent in the residual dualism of Plato's own thought.

Be that as it may, the world of nature in Plato's thought is never degraded to being the lifeless, soulless, mechanical thing that it becomes in the thought of the seventeenth century pioneers of modern science. It is always, as it is for the Pythagoreans and the earlier Ionian philosophers, something 'ensouled', *empsychon*, a living organism or animal, within which are lesser organisms possessing souls of their own; so that a flower or a bird or a rock is both a living organism in itself and also part of the great living organism which is the world. And just as the world of nature is a material organism, alive everywhere, so the intelligible world

3. *Sophist*, 248E.

is an immaterial organism, also alive everywhere by virtue of the fact that its forms are dynamically related to each other, each having dialectical connections with the others.

The *Timaeus* also expresses the idea of a cosmic God which was so to dominate the Hellenistic world. This God is the Demiurge, the maker or craftsman that fashions the sensible world upon the pre-existing model of the eternal forms of the intelligible world. In this respect he is not so much a rival and distinct power as a mythical double of the World Soul. Moreover, he is in some sense an external and impersonal God. He is not personal and interior. The importance of this becomes apparent when the place of man in the cosmos and his relationship with the divine are considered.

For the Plato of the *Timaeus*, man is not envisaged as a creature whose full reality depends upon his relationship with a personal God. The relationship of man and God is not a personal relationship, complete in itself, a mutual reciprocity between the one and the other. Nor is this relationship any more personal for the Hellenistic sages. The God of the Hellenistic sages is essentially a God of the cosmos. Man is a part of the cosmos. Divorced from the cosmos, he has no real existence. This is in keeping with the dominant trend of the philosophy of the city states.

For the fifth and fourth centuries BC, man is first of all a member of the city, the *polis*. It is only within the larger unit of the city that he achieves his proper status. It is membership of the city that distinguishes him from the animals; or at least membership of a city is proof of that element of reason in him which distinguishes him from the animals. He calls himself a political animal, a *zoon politikon*. It is only from this point of view that one can understand the dread and the severity of banishment from the city. To be banished from the city is to be deprived of human status; it is to be prevented from communion in all that gives human life value. Outside the city there is no fully human life.

At the end of the fourth century BC, after the breakdown of the city state, man's existence as a citizen did not fundamentally change, but now, instead of being a member of a local city, he became a member of a cosmic city. But apart from the cosmic city he still has no real existence. He is still but a part of a more important whole and his destiny can be achieved only by subordinating himself to the whole. The whole is a Living Being, a God, who is far superior to man. The world, the cosmic city, possesses a soul. It is obedient to the order of God. Man is good or bad in so far as he submits himself to and identifies himself with the divine order of the

15

cosmos. The order of the cosmos is something external to and independent of him. God Himself is self-sufficient without man. What is
important for God is not the single person but the whole. In the time of
the city state, what had been important was not the prosperity of the
single person but the prosperity of the city. Now what is important is the
cosmic order. This the single person could in no essential way disturb.
His part is to learn the divine plan, to obey it, to adjust himself to it, to
become one with the cosmic order. But whether he does or does not is a
matter of indifference to the order itself. The order itself simply is; man
has not made it and it is outside him. It is eternal and complete. Even if
there was no man, the cosmos would still be what it is, realized, complete,
beautiful and everlasting.

Stoicism carried some of these tendencies to their limit. Like Plato, the
Stoics saw the cosmos as a great living organism—living because it is
ensouled. This Soul is a fine, fiery substance, a spirit or breath that
penetrates and pervades the whole cosmic body, holding together and
unifying the elements that compose each thing. One thing differs from
another only according to the degree to which it is penetrated by this
spirit or breath, the divine or seed-sowing Logos (*Logos spermatikos*).
There is more Logos in some things than in others. There is more Logos
in man than in a stone—indeed, man's soul is a 'spark' or modality of the
divine Logos itself.

Yet these differences are differences of degree, not of quality. All in the
universe is linked together by the presence within everything of the
divine Logos, also called Zeus, or Fate, or God, that binds the world into
one integrated system and predetermines all events according to a
providential order. All lives, moves and has its being within this
universal spirit. The world is an organic whole; and the history of the
world is an unbroken chain in which everything, past and future, human
and cosmic, is inextricably involved.

Yet this process is not only essentially impersonal where man is
concerned; it is also inescapable. For though for the Stoics the dualism in
Plato's thought that derives from the radical contrast between Being and
Becoming, between the non-physical and the physical, disappears, and
the world is envisaged as self-contained and self-renewing, what this also
signifies is the loss of any recognition of a transcendent spiritual order of
reality beyond this visible world-order. As a consequence man is forced
to regard himself as inevitably and inextricably in bondage to the
impersonal, materialized and embodied form of existence in which he is

16

involved. It is true that he is called upon to realize his affinity and oneness with the divine Logos; but this does not mean that thereby he could achieve a personal liberation or self-deliverance from the changes and chances of this mortal life. All he could achieve was a state of noble indifference or unruffled impassivity in the face of all that happens, for good or ill, for joy or sorrow, in the prison-house in which he is subjected to forces entirely beyond his control.

The logical outcome of this is an enormous sense of fatality, a sense of helplessness and oppression before the world-system. Such a sense might be mitigated, if it could not be overcome, by identifying Fate with Providence: what is is for the best. Or it could give rise, as it did in the case of the Gnostics, to a view of things that went to the other extreme: to positing a totally disembodied, extra-terrestrial, pure God, removed as far as possible from all contact with or regard for the world and for the God of Fate who ruled over it. In other words, it could give rise to a dualism even more extreme than that of the Plato of the *Phaedo* and the *Republic*.

It is in the collection of writings known as the *Corpus Hermeticum*[4] that the two sides of Plato of which we have spoken, meet. They do not meet to be reconciled. These Hermetic texts do not present a new synthesis. The dualism of intelligible and sensible, of soul and body, is proclaimed as strongly as ever. 'There are two sorts of things, the corporeal and the incorporeal; that which is mortal is of the one sort, and that which is divine is of another sort.'[5] Or again: 'The cosmos is one mass of evil.'[6] The value of the sensible world and its participation in the divine is denied: 'For all things that come into being are full of per-turbations, seeing that the very process of coming into being involves perturbation. But wherever there is perturbation, there the Good cannot be.'[7] Concrete reality is illusion. What is real is 'that which is not sullied by matter . . . nor limited by boundaries, that which has no colour and no shape, that which is without integument, and is luminous, that which is apprehended by itself alone, that which is changeless and unalterable'.[8]

---

4. A collection of sacred texts, partly Oriental in tendency, partly Stoic and partly an offshoot of ancient Greek philosophy, compiled in late antiquity and attributed to Hermes Trismegistus, as Thoth, the Egyptian god of wisdom, was designated. All quotations from these texts are from: *Corpus Hermeticum*, edited and translated by Walter Scott (Oxford, 1924).

5. *Corpus Hermeticum*, op. cit, Lib: iv.6.   6. Ibid, Lib. vi:4.

7. Ibid, Lib. vi:2.   8. Ibid, Lib. xiii:6.

The body is an obstacle to knowledge of God; it must be discarded, denied, rejected: 'But first you must tear off this garment which you wear—this cloak of darkness, this web of ignorance, this prop of evil, this bond of corruption—this living death, this conscious corpse, this tomb you carry about with you—this robber in the house, this enemy who hates the things you seek after, and grudges you the things which you desire.'[9]

Thus on the one hand the authors of some of the *Hermetica* subscribe to a complete sense-denying ethic; they exalt the transcendental at the expense of the earthly; they attack the primal instincts of man, and bid man free himself from them; they endorse and emphasize the negative and evil character of the world of matter, and of man in so far as he is part of the world of matter; they would have man sacrifice what is natural and earthly in himself to the impersonal, objectivized and transcendental Good, to the intelligible world.

On the other hand there are passages in the *Corpus Hermeticum* which affirm the participation of the sensible world in the divine world in a way far more positive than that in which the *Timaeus* affirms it. Life is not a nightmare only, the world is not a barren nothing, the kingdom of shadows: 'God is the source of all that is; He is the source of mind, and of nature, and of matter. To show forth His wisdom has He made all things; for He is the source of all.'[10] It is 'in God that nature has her being'.[11] The sensible, changing world is also part of an invisible, unmoving reality: 'God, who is unmoved, moves in all that moves, and Him who is hidden is made manifest through His works.'[12] God is ever making 'all things, in heaven, in air, on earth, and in the deep, in every part of the cosmos, in all that is and in all that is not. For in all this there is nothing that He is not. He is both the things that are, and the things that are not'.[13]

God—Reality—is both one and many. He is a unity-in-difference, an incorporeal corporality:

He is hidden, yet most manifest. He is apprehensible by thought alone, yet we can see Him with our eyes. He is bodiless, yet has many bodies, or rather, is embodied in all bodies. There is nothing that He is not; for all things that exist are even He. For this reason all names are names of Him, because all things come from Him, their one Father; and for this reason He has no name, because He is the Father of all.[14]

9. Ibid, Lib. VII:2.   10. Ibid, Lib. III:1.   11. Ibid, Lib. III:1.
12. Ibid, Lib. V:5.   13. Ibid, Lib. V:9.   14. Ibid, Lib. V:10.

It is an echo of the Psalmist's: 'If I ascend into heaven, Thou art there: if I make my bed in hell, behold, Thou art there. If I take the wings of the morning, and dwell in the uttermost parts of the sea, even there shall Thy hand lead me.'[15]

It is in a passage which speaks of man's erotic energies that most reveals how far at times the authors of the *Hermetica* can pass beyond the dualist point of view, beyond the objectivization and impersonality of the Greek and Hellenistic philosophical tradition, and reach an understanding of reality which escapes such categories. The erotic energies are often those most readily attacked in a sense-denying, dualistic ethic: the image of Eros 'crucified' stands above much of this type of morality. The *Hermetica* in the following passage go beyond this stance: they link the erotic passions to the highest processes of life, seeing them as manifestations of divine energy itself:

And in that conjunction of the two sexes, or, to speak more truly, that fusion of them into one, which may be rightly named Eros, or Aphrodite, or both at once, there is a deeper meaning than man can comprehend. It is a truth to be accepted as sure and evident above all other truths, that by God, the Master of all generative power, has been devised and bestowed upon all creatures this sacrament of eternal reproduction, with all the affection, all the joy and gladness, all the yearning and heavenly love that are inherent in its being. And there were need that I should tell of the compelling force with which this sacrament binds man and woman together, were it not that each of us, if he directs his thought upon himself, can learn it from his inmost feeling.[16]

It would be a mistake to emphasize too greatly this break in some of the Hermetic texts with the more dualistic side of Greek and Hellenistic philosophy. It need only be pointed out that such a break is implicit in certain passages of the *Hermetica*. But in general the *Hermetica* continue the objectivized impersonal tradition which descends from Plato and whose course we have briefly glanced at. Thus on the one hand they reassert the dualism of the Plato of the *Phaedo*, the *Symposium*, and the *Republic*. But on the other hand they also express that vision of the organic wholeness of life, of the intermingling of sensible and intelligible,

15. Psalm 139.
16. *Corpus Hermeticum*, op. cit, Asclep. III:21.

visible and invisible, which is suggested in Plato's *Timaeus* and in some aspects of Stoicism. Supreme Reality does not exclude the world of the senses; Reality is present in the forms of nature itself: It is not opposed to creation. Both form and matter, the ever-active consciousness and the passive non-consciousness, are aspects of this single Reality, that is everywhere and in everything:

> Everywhere God will come to meet you, everywhere He will appear to you, at places and times at which you look not for it, in your waking hours and in your sleep, when you are journeying by water and by land, in the night time and in the day time, when you are speaking and when you are silent; for there is nothing which is not God. And do you say 'God is invisible'? Speak not so. Who is more manifest than God? For this very purpose He has made all things, that through all things you may see Him. This is God's goodness, that He manifests Himself through all things. Nothing is invisible, not even an incorporeal thing; mind is seen in its thinking, and God in His working. [17]

The great break with the impersonality and objectivization of Greek and Hellenistic philosophy, with its emphasis on the exterior cosmic order and its worship of a God who regulates and controls this order, comes of course with Christianity. The accent is shifted from the outer to the inner, from the impersonal to the personal, onto the internal struggle and stress of the human soul. With Christianity the single individual, the human person, is brought face to face, not with some impersonal Absolute, but with an equally living Person, the tri-personal God.

Christianity gave to the human individual the sense that within himself, as a single being, and quite apart from any city or cosmic order, the deepest mysteries of life are to be found: the supranatural dwells within. He is no longer asked to sacrifice himself to any larger, more important but more impersonal whole in order to achieve his destiny. He is, potentially, himself the whole. His task is to penetrate into his own inner depths where he can encounter and unite with that Other who is both the source and the most real aspect of his own personality. As a particular, individual person he has the capacity to be an instance or an embodiment of the full reality of the divine. He can attain full deification, in both soul and body. The body is not excluded from this process. Matter

17. Ibid, Lib. XI:22.

is not evil. It, too, is created by God and possesses an intrinsic spiritual disposition and aspiration.

In the Christian mystery, as it is interpreted by the great masters of the Christian contemplative tradition, the last traces of the impersonal and objectivized character of classical theology which are still present in the thought of Plotinus are eliminated, and the whole drama of human life is focused on an inner, intimate, intensely personal exchange between the human individual and God, between the human creature and the uncreated Light. It is a drama that takes place within the depths of the individual human soul. And the most fertile scene for its enactment is thought to be, not the city, but the desert.[18]

This understanding of things derives from a particular view of man and of human destiny. In this view, man is not simply a mortal being with a destiny confined to the material world. He is also created in the image of God. He possesses a spiritual identity as well as a psychic and physical identity. As a spiritual identity he transcends the psychic and physical worlds and the laws that apply to them. He is an inhabitant of eternity, superior to fate and necessity. It is only as a mortal creature, or in so far as he is a mortal creature, that he is subject to fate and necessity and to psychic and physical laws. And he has become subject in this way as a result of his declension from his spiritual state. Through his fall he has entered into a world subject to corruption and mortality, a world disfigured as a consequence of his own spiritual lapse. So long as he remains, where his conscious awareness and experience are concerned, within the limits of this world, he remains bound to and victim of forces he is powerless to control except in a very restricted way. But if, after struggle and purification, he raises the level of his consciousness and experience—or allows them to be raised—to the world of eternity, he may then realize his spiritual identity, an identity over which death and the laws of the psychic and physical worlds cease to have dominion.

This view of things presents us with what we might call the great contradiction, the decisive either-or of life. The recognition that our being is rooted in a reality that transcends the psychic and physical worlds and all natural necessity, and that we are heirs to eternity and not simply mortal creatures, at the same time demands that we acknowledge

18. See *The Desert is Alive*, ed. Graeme Ferguson and John Chryssavgis (Melbourne, 1990), where references to works on the spirituality of the desert are given in the notes to the various contributions.

something that is beyond the immediate grasp of both our senses and our mind. That we belong to the psychic and physical worlds is something that our senses and our mind can tell us. That we belong to the kingdom of God neither our senses nor our mind, working on sensory observation or conceptual representation, can verify. Indeed, the fact that we so evidently belong to the psychic and physical worlds, so evidently suffer the same organic processes of growth and decay that the mortal world suffers, might well seem to preclude the likelihood that we may also belong to another world in which these processes are transcended. This is a contradiction which those whose vision of things is limited to the psychic and physical worlds do not have to confront.

It is a contradiction which Christians confront through the symbol of the Cross. The Cross stands at the junction of our two-fold identity, at the parting of the ways between the mortal and the immortal worlds. It stands over the abyss which opens out beyond the limits of our sensory and mental reach. At this point, sensory reaction and logical representation give place to something else. They give place to the recognition of a higher reality. We begin the way of the Cross when we recognize that we belong to this reality which neither the senses nor the human mind can by themselves grasp. Sensory reaction and conceptual representation halt at the frontiers of the psychic and physical worlds. Here stands the Cross, symbol of the contradiction and also of the resolution of the contradiction. We complete the way of the Cross when we transcend our merely mortal state and re-awaken to our spiritual life in eternity. The way is one that we travel not with the dialectic of logic, but through the paradoxes of mystical faith. It is also one which leads us through the experience of death.

The ancient world also had its sense of this significance of death which lies at the centre of Christianity. 'Mortals are immortals and immortals are mortals, the one living the other's death and dying the other's life', said Herakleitos.[19] Plato speaks of philosophy as a study in dying.[20] In the ancient Mysteries there is an awareness that in the depths of the human soul a drama may be played out in which man, through an experience which he likens to dying, changes his state of mortality for one of immortality. The myth in which the ancient world most fully imaged this drama was that of the suffering and dying god, of the god who dies to be born again. Through an imitation of this myth in terms of

19. Herakleitos, fr. 62.   20. *Phaedo*, 61 b–69 e.

his own personal life the initiate into the Mysteries might achieve rebirth. Through death he might achieve liberation. Death meant not physical decomposition but the overcoming of the tyranny of the ego. The ego as the centre of things must die to open the way to a new and more fertile life. This is to be realized through an *ekstasis*, a standing outside oneself. But how?

By a concentration and gathering together of the powers of the soul, was the answer that Plato gave.[21] Plato also indicated other means. The ego might be overcome through a mania which destroys for a moment the physical balance of man and overwhelms his self-conscious faculties—a possession 'which comes not from mortal weakness or disease but from a divine banishment of the commonplace'.[22] In an intimate relationship, in a vital union with his god, the initiate participates in another life. The rites of the various Mysteries give the pattern of the mystic drama, a divine progress which is the principle and prototype of salvation. The initiate has to re-enact this progress in his own life. Thus he brings to birth in himself the state of soul, the comprehension, to which its images and symbols correspond. He is conducted beyond his normal, everyday consciousness of himself. Like Apuleius, he has to 'touch the frontiers of death'; he has to 'tread the threshold of Persephone'.[23] Through sharing the earthly trials of the god, he might at last partake also of the god's celestial happiness. The Mysteries, turning the will towards the divine and exalting the interior spirit, might not have much obvious social use. But they could answer to aspirations of a far deeper nature. They gave, by sudden illumination, foretaste of a numinous reality of which the intensity turned to little worth the fortunes and favours of this world.

The ancient Mysteries have been called imitative anticipations of the Christian mystery. Quite how much they were anticipations can be seen from phrases of Christ like: 'Verily, verily, I say unto you, except a corn of wheat fall into the earth and die, it abides alone; but if it die, it brings forth much fruit.'[24] Or from phrases of St Paul like: 'How are the dead raised up? With what body do they come? Thou fool, that which thou sowest is not quickened except it die—it is sown in corruption, it is raised in incorruption.'[25]

21. *Phaedo*, 80E. 22. *Phaedrus*, 265A. See also *Phaedrus*, 244B ff.
23. Apuleius, *The Golden Ass*, Bk. II, chap. 48. 24. John 12:24.
25. I Cor. 15:35–36, 42.

Yet in spite of similarities there are crucial differences between the ancient Mysteries and the Christian mystery. To start with, the god of the Mysteries is not an active god. He is a passive god. There might be a movement of man towards him; he might allow man in moments of rapture and *ekstasis* to take possession of him. But he does not himself move towards man; he does not himself actively love man or enter into the complexity of his nature. There is no incarnation, no interpenetration of the divine and the human, no divine compassion.

Second, there is in Christianity a new attitude towards suffering. The ancient attitude to suffering also tended to be a passive, a negative attitude. A case in point is that of Odysseus. Many things, pleasant and unpleasant, happen to Odysseus. But they happen to him because he cannot help it. Had he known how, he would have gone straight back to Ithaca. Unfortunately, the gods willed otherwise. He has to suffer. Through suffering he might perhaps learn wisdom, but this is fortuitous. Wisdom in any case lay in the voluntary submission to the workings of an impersonal fate. Fate is just but impersonal. Even Zeus is powerless before fate, which in the end brings all things to completion.

Christ's attitude is the opposite to this. He gives the myth of the wounded and dying god a new significance. He does not simply endure what happens to Him, passively. Christ through His own choice enters into suffering as a way to spiritual liberation. Suffering is something positive. What gives pain and distress in the world is so excellent a way to spiritual fulfilment that God Himself undergoes the most shameful of deaths so that man may understand this.

The prototype of the Christian mystery is the figure of the God-man, the Theanthropos, the figure who, in the words of one of the Church offices, 'as a being made of earth has suffered in the flesh and yet as God has remained without suffering and who in Himself has transformed corruption into incorruption and through His Resurrection has opened the well of immortal life.'[26] It is to this that St Paul refers when he asks: 'Has not God made foolish the wisdom of this world?'—he means the wisdom of the Hellenic philosophers—and says that the foolishness of God is wiser than men and the weakness of God is stronger than men.[27] In the Christian mystery it is the Divinity Himself who, under the figure of a servant, drains the cup of human suffering, only in the end to defeat

26. Morning Service for the Saturday of Holy Week.
27. I Cor, 1 : 20, 25.

suffering; who, emptying Himself of His divine nature, enters into death, only in the end to tread death underfoot. It is this victory, the victory of the Cross and the triumph over death, that we are asked to imitate.

Yet this imitation does not mean the negation of created human nature. Here we touch a third difference between the ancient Mysteries and the Christian mystery. The goal proposed for the initiate into the Mysteries is one that involves the surrender of the separated human consciousness. It is one that involves an *ekstasis*, the standing out of and beyond a consciousness of an individual personal identity, of the whole man. It means an abandoning and transcending of created human nature and a sinking and merging into the undifferentiated unity of the divine Principle. The same goal is proposed by the more metaphysical philosophers, by the Platonists and the Neoplatonists. When Plotinus spoke of the divine Principle as 'a presence overpassing all knowledge' and of the way to it as a going 'beyond knowing', as a 'flight of the alone to the alone',[28] this presence of which he speaks is still something impersonal, an absolute simplicity or a God-unity; and its realization on the part of the human individual means a corresponding overcoming of his consciousness of himself as a separated being, distinct from all other beings. It means an overcoming of all multiplicity and differentiation, and therefore of all created and personal categories.

For the Christians, too, God transcends the limits of human knowledge. But He is not simply a First Cause or a primordial Unity. Nor is He, as Plato tended to see Him, an impersonal mathematical ideal, His mind filled with pure geometrical forms. On the contrary, He is a living power, the God 'who makes the darkness His secret place';[29] and the qualities that most manifest His nature are qualities such as love, joy, fulness of being, immortality, compassion, tenderness, peace and so on, all of which by definition escape the net of number and geometrical form. He may even be moved to weep, just as He may also be moved to wrath. And it is such qualities that also most typify the true nature of human beings, who are His offspring, created in His image, and whom He embraces in His own being, along with the whole multiplicity and diversity of the world He has brought forth.

The Christian initiate, then, is not asked to abandon his separate

28. *Ennead* VI:9. See also *Enneads* I:7: V:5; VI:9.
29. Cf. Psalm 18.

personal identity. He is not asked to sink himself into the undifferentiated simplicity of the One or into the contemplation of an abstract non-human world. It is not his purpose to disappear into the abyss of mystery. The purpose of the Christian way is the divinization of man. 'Not from the beginning were we made gods,' said St Irenaeus, 'but first indeed men, and then finally gods.' 'He became man in order to divinize us,' said St Athanasios speaking of Christ's work. God united Himself to human nature, said St Gregory of Nazianzos, 'so that I, too, might be made God'. The Incarnation, said St Maximos the Confessor, 'makes God a man through the deification of man, and man a god through the humanization of God'.[30] This is the significance of the summons to be born again, the significance of the triumph over death: that man must recreate himself into the image of God in which he is created and which, however obscured, lies still in the depths of his being. He must recover his spiritual identity.

Nor is it his purpose to recover it by ceasing to be human. On the contrary, it is only through this divinization that he realizes his destiny as a unique created being, as a unique human being. There is a reciprocity between God and man, the uncreated and the created. There is a sense of God as a man 'seen with our eyes and with our hands handled'.[31] God is born in man and man is born in God. The humanity remains within the divinity, the divinity within the humanity. We are not asked to abandon our created human nature. We are asked to purify this nature, to free it from alien impersonal accretions, psychical and physical, but not to destroy it or to eliminate it. The passions themselves are not to be eradicated. They are to be reorientated, redirected. The body of man, as well as the soul, has a spiritual disposition. It, too, is capable of experiencing the divine, it, too, is capable of being deified along with the soul.[32] Nothing of the living person, of the unique creature, is to be sacrificed.

By a gradual process of purification and illumination—an initiation which in many ways resembles that of the old Mysteries—man is to become as God. It is this idea of divine-human collaboration, of a real

---

30. St Irenaeus, *Adv. Haereses*, V, P.G. 7, 1120; St Athanasios, *De incarnatione Verbi*, cap. 54, P.G.25, 192; St Gregory of Nazianzos, *Third Theological Discourse*, 19; St Maximos the Confessor, *Ambigua*, P.G. 91, 1084CD.

31. Epistle of St John, 1:1.

32. See St Maximos the Confessor, *Texts on Theology* II, 88, P.G.90, 1168A. See *The Philokalia*, vol. 2 (London, 1990), p.160.

effective partnership between the free creature and the Creator, that is at the basis of the Christian mystery. 'And we shall become as gods, joined in intimacy to God, showing no stain on our body but all being in likeness to the whole body of Christ, each one of us having as our limbs the complete Christ. For the One is made many, and the One yet remains undivided, but each part is indeed the whole Christ.'[33] In these words St Simeon the New Theologian expresses the supreme realization of the Christian faith. He expresses the consummation of that triumph over death of which the Cross is the symbol.

Yet at the same time as they stressed the essentially inner and personal relationship between God and man, Christian apologists could not ignore the cosmological implications of their revelation. For this revelation has made it clear that not only man but all creation—everything in the heavens and on earth—is capable of being restored to its pristine, incorruptible glory in the divine world from which it originally proceeds.[34] But if the glorified Christ is to include and sum up in Himself the whole of creation, then He must really and organically be part of that creation. He has as it were to straddle the gulf between the natural and the divine in His own being.

Hence the vital importance of affirming the full reality of the incarnation of the divine in Christ, and the constant warfare of early Christian apologists against those, such as the Gnostics and the Docetists, who tended to minimize or outrightly to deny its reality. For, it was felt, to lose touch with this reality would be to lose touch with the full reality not only of human salvation but also of the fulfilment of the whole natural order, which waited with earnest expectation for the revelation of the sons of God.[35]

This presented Christian apologists with the task of giving an intelligible account of how a God who, as their revelation also made clear, is absolutely transcendent to His creation, can also be present within it. This in effect is the same task as that which in Platonic terms is seen as giving an explanation of the relationship between Being and Becoming that does not lead to the conclusion that Being is excluded from the world of Becoming and that there is a radical hiatus between the two. And it was precisely in such terms that the early Christian apologists who attempted

33. St Simeon the New Theologian, P.G. 120, 532 BC.

34. Cf. Eph. 1:9–10.

35. Cf. Rom. 8:19. See also in this connection D. S. Wallace-Hadrill, *The Greek Patristic View of Nature* (Manchester, 1968), pp. 110–30.

to wrestle with this issue—St Justin Martyr (c100–c165), St Irenaeus (c130–c200) and the Alexandrians St Clement (c150–c215) and Origen (c185–c254)—tended to see it.

It was consequently in ways which have Platonic connotations that they also tended to make this issue intelligible.[36] God, like Pure Being, is immaterial, without figure or shape, impassible, incapable of being declared. Yet Christian scriptures also make it clear that God creates the world and that He creates it in and through His Logos, who is also fully divine. Hence Christ, the Logos incarnate, is the instrumental cause of creation, the one 'in whom all things consist'.[37] This means that Christ, the Logos incarnate, has a mediatorial cosmic role: He mediates between the immaterial transcendent Being of God and the world of material realities—the world of nature—and in His divine-human Person He embraces both. This is to assimilate, to some extent at least, Christ's role to the role of the World Soul in Platonic thought, for the Platonic World Soul also has a cosmic mediatorial role between the world of Being and that of Becoming similar to that assigned by these early Christian theologians to the Logos.

Yet there is a further implication of this which is of the utmost significance. God creates the world in and through His Logos. The Logos is thus the first expression of the abundant creativity by means of which God moves out of His self-enclosed and utterly transcendent isolation, the first expression of the virtualities latent in the unsoundable depths of God's Being. He is God's Intelligence-content, containing in Himself in an invisible way the exemplars or archetypes of all created existence. At the same time He is the mediating principle through which these exemplars or archetypes are made manifest in the visible world, the active and immanent agent of a descending and progressively diversifying stream of existence. The Logos and the visible world are thus correlative in the economy of the divine creation. The Logos is the presence in the world of the Godhead itself.

Thus by definition the world of Becoming can and does participate in the world of Being, corruptible nature in incorruptible life. The ingenerate, immaterial, transcendent God is present in and with the generate

36. For a full exploration of the early Christian theology of which what is given here is a brief summary, see Richard A. Norris, *God and the World in Early Christian Theology* (London, 1966), pp. 33–80 and pp. 106–29.

37. Col. 1:17.

world He has created. One cannot therefore think of God without simultaneously thinking of the world in which He reveals or manifests Himself: the one implies the other. And this is the case quite apart from any moment we can envisage in terms of historical time. The Logos is the power through which God creates the world; He is God's unlimited creative power. And this power is eternally begotten in its full reality.

It is impossible consequently to conceive of a time in which this creativity of the Logos is not engaged, and in which the Logos is not present and immanent in the acts and effects—namely, God's works and creatures—through which He is manifest. Not only must such created effects always exist, but the Logos must always manifest Himself in them. The Logos is active from beginning to end of the whole eternal creative process. In the person of the historical Christ He mediates the divine revelation. But He is also the trans-historical mode of God's eternal relationship with His creation, eternally incarnate in every aspect of it. The doctrine of eternal creation, and of God's immanence in this creation, is a correlate of the understanding of the divine nature itself.

In the Christian perspective, then, visible nature—*natura naturata* —is not evil. On the contrary, everything that exists participates, simply by virtue of the fact that it does exist, in the creative energies of the highest life of all. These energies are the creative wills of God, dynamic and intentional. They are present in the physical world. Everything created has its point of contact with the spiritual world and possesses its own individual consciousness. When things live and act in accordance with their natural, intrinsic nature, they live and act within a relationship of mutual harmony established by the fact that their own being is rooted in the Being of God, source of all harmony.

That this harmony is only too often disrupted in the actual conditions of this world is not therefore, in the Christian view, due to any essential defect or deficiency in nature itself, or to the activity of any power of evil inherent in it. It is due to a prior breach in the relationship between man and God whereby man has fallen from the order of life to which by nature he belongs; and as a consequence of this lapse an element of discord and disruption has been introduced into the whole created world. 'All creation sighs and throbs with pain', wrote St Paul,[38] referring to the plight of the natural order consequent upon man's failure to maintain his

38. Rom. 8:22.

spiritual integrity. It is because man has dishonoured the divine image within him that the original cosmic harmony has been ruptured.[39]

That is why, when rightly conceived and experienced, this understanding of things induces in man a great compassion for the whole of creation on account of the cruelty and suffering that afflict it. Such compassion may seem excessive to us, who take our presence and present condition in the world of visible nature for granted and may feel responsible for particular injuries within it, but not for its tragic state itself. 'What is a compassionate heart?' asks St Isaac of Nineveh; and he answers: 'It is a heart that burns with compassion for the whole of creation—for men, for birds, for beasts, for demons, for all creatures. He who has this heart cannot call to mind or see one creature without his eyes filling with tears because of the immense compassion which seizes his heart.'[40]

Yet this compassion does not mean an attitude of passivity before the fate that has overtaken visible nature and man in their fallen state. It does not lead to a mystique of submission and obedience to the consequences of man's lapse. Rather is it a summons to us to remake our spiritual state, to restore that harmony of creation which has been disrupted by our loss of this state. Unless it leads us first to achieve the integrity of our own being our compassion may only too easily become but a vain self-flattering sentimentality and may produce more evil than it seeks to eliminate. And to achieve this integrity we must raise our consciousness—or allow it to be raised—beyond the limits of visible nature. We must reaffirm our roots in a reality that transcends visible nature, that transcends all necessity and even death itself.

Yet although in this manner these early Christian theologians attempted to bridge the gap between God and the world, Being and Becoming, which in Platonic thought is never totally eliminated, other theologians even in the early period, and to a far greater extent in the later mediaeval period, did allow themselves to be inveigled by a form of dualism similar to that always latent in Platonic thought; and this led to a negative and depreciatory attitude to the world as it is experienced through the senses. A fuller analysis of the preconceptions that lay behind this attitude is

39. An attempt to analyse more fully the cause and consequences of man's loss of his spiritual integrity is made in the final chapter of this book.

40. Isaac of Nineveh, *Mystic Treatises*, trs. A. J. Wensinck (Amsterdam, 1923), p.341.

reserved for the final chapter of this book. Here all that it is necessary to say is that by and large in later mediaeval Christian thought there is a progressive devaluation of the cosmos, an increasing tendency to envisage the Divinity as withdrawn from the natural world: the cosmos is 'demystified', robbed of its divine quality. The elements of the cosmos—water, earth, fire, air—tend to be seen as controlled by spirits hostile to God rather than as modes of God's self-expression and as guided by Him. The transcendent is exalted at the expense of the sense-world, the invisible at the expense of the visible. The understanding of the trans-historical and cosmic dimension of the incarnation of the divine Logos is progressively eclipsed.

It is true that at least in so far as Greek patristic theology is concerned creation in its original state is said to be good and to represent a series of divine theophanies; and even in its fallen state it is seen to present forms whose contemplation may lead the mind back to an awareness of divine beauty. But only too often, and particularly in the line of theology that stems from St Augustine, the sensible world in itself is regarded as little more than a 'lump of perdition' and as handed over to the forces of evil. Hence Christian asceticism based on such an attitude demanded a rejection of this world, its abandonment in favour of a supra-sensible world. In the sphere of the senses and of the passions and instincts the devil is active. The purpose of the devil is to prevent the soul's union with God. Consequently, the first step towards such a union is the mortification and even extirpation of the passions and an often vicious denigration of sensual or aesthetic enjoyment, with a corresponding effort to sever the ties that link man as a created being to the cosmos.

Christianity tended to become increasingly other-worldly. In a way totally at odds with its own revelation, it increasingly sundered the order of human salvation from the order of nature, human destiny from the destiny of nature, until in the end the one could be regarded as entirely independent of the other and only the first as of any real significance. Even the distinction made by the scholastic philosophers between the order of faith, which pertains to the supranatural world, and the order of reason, which pertains to the natural world, with the corresponding distinction between formal and efficient causes, can be made only when the mind has lost its grasp of the truth, when its spiritual or higher consciousness is eclipsed, and when it has reduced itself to accepting a doctrine of creation, or a cosmology, that is as truncated as it is misconceived.

If this cosmology did not formally stipulate an unbridgeable ontological gulf between the ultimate transcendent ground of Being and the manifold forms of created life as these are manifest in all their munificent abundance, it increasingly failed to affirm in an unambiguous manner that the inner and immortal Self—the transcendent God—and the source of the great cosmic energies are one and the same, or that the transcendent One and the changing multitudinous world of the senses constitute a single undivided and indivisible reality. It would be hard if not impossible to find, for instance, in the whole body of mediaeval Christian theology anything that remotely corresponds to the passage on the potentially sacramental nature of the erotic relationship which was cited above from the *Corpus Hermeticum*.[41]

It was against what tended to be this inadequate and even deficient attitude to cosmological issues in later mediaeval Christian theology that the Renaissance, initially at least, represented a reaction. For, initially at least, this reaction took the form of an attempt to give the natural world a positive status within the cosmological scheme of things, to validate the realities which we experience through the senses, and to affirm the centrality of man to and in the flux and reflux of natural processes. Why this intellectual revolt should have resulted in a world-view in which nature is degraded to being regarded as something soulless, impersonal and mechanical, and man as little more than an insignificant observer of a vast cosmic process that goes on outside him and independently of him, will, I hope, become clear in the following chapter.

41. See also on this theme my *Christianity and Eros* (London, 1976), and the chapter entitled 'The Nuptial Mystagogy' in my *The Sacred in Life and Art* (Ipswich, 1990), pp. 108–28.

2 The Fetish of Mathematics and the Iconoclasm of Modern Science

In the previous chapter I have attempted to indicate some of the main features that characterize the world image —the cosmology—and the human image—the anthropology —effective for the European consciousness down to the time of the Renaissance; and in so doing I have pointed towards certain possible limitations in the Christian understanding of creation, particularly in the later mediaeval world, that were to provoke crucial reactions. Yet whatever these limitations may have been, and however justified the criticisms they provoked, the mediaeval Christian consciousness was still permeated by the sense of the sacredness of man and nature. The human and the cosmic images effective for it were still sacred paradigms. As I have written elsewhere,[1] the mediaeval Christian world was an organically integrated world—a sacred order established by God in which everything, not only man and man's artefacts, but every living form of plant, bird or animal, the sun, moon and stars, the waters and the mountains were seen as signs of things sacred (*signa rei sacra*), expressions of a divine harmony, symbols linking the visible and the invisible, earth and heaven. The world about us is a world rich in colour and sound, in love and beauty, speaking everywhere of this purposive harmony and harmonious purpose.

Ultimately these purposes are supra-terrestrial, non-temporal and

1. See my *The Rape of Man and Nature* (Ipswich, 1987), p.64. See also on this theme C.S. Lewis, *The Discarded Image* (Cambridge, 1976), pp.92ff.

spiritual. God is not only the Creator of everything: He is also the consummation of everything. Whatever harmony might be perceived in this world—the world of nature—is but a mirror. It is a means to a deeper harmony, to a knowledge and an enjoyment of living beings of a higher order, who in their turn mirror and transmit the love and beauty of God and who thus complete the divine circuit, the final consummation: to know God and to enjoy Him eternally. God Himself has no purpose: He is the ultimate subject of all purposes.

Given that this spiritual universe constituted the birthright of all people belonging to the European world down at least to the time of the Renaissance, we are faced with these questions: How in the space of a few hundred years have we achieved a state of mind so dominated by abstract, impersonal, materialist and quantitative concepts and values that we can to all intents and purposes use and abuse ourselves and the world of nature—or connive in their use and abuse—as if they were equally abstract, impersonal, non-sacred and soulless? What new paradigm of thought has so insinuated itself into us that it has imposed upon us a self-view and a world-view that are as merciless as they are non-spiritual? How have we so destroyed the sacred images of man and nature that our societies are now little more than battlegrounds for the secular free-for-all of the lowest common denominators?

The answer to these questions in a succinct, even if over-simplified, form lies in the character of the modern scientific revolution accomplished between the sixteenth and eighteenth centuries, and in the paradigm of thought that was its brain-child. This paradigm has increasingly dominated the European mentality for over the last two hundred years and more, and has increasingly dominated the mentality of other peoples in the world over the last hundred years; and it is this paradigm which has been responsible not only for directing the course of modern scientific theory and practice, but also for producing the modern industrial and technological inferno and so for producing our present state of crisis. The revolution that consummated it has been described by one of its most astute analysts as 'the most successful movement of thought that history so far records', and as 'an unprecedented intellectual revolution'.[2]

2. See E.A.Burtt, *The Metaphysical Foundations of Modern Science* (London, 1980), pp.207–8. Although I do not share the author's evaluation of what he analyses with such clarity in this book, I am considerably indebted in what follows to the analysis itself.

Such tributes may represent excusable hyperbole. But we do have to remember that the pioneers of this revolution—men like Kepler, Galileo, Descartes and Newton, to name but four of them—did not simply have to replace one set of theories by another set. They had to destroy one world and replace it by another. They had to destroy one conceptual framework of the mind and replace it by another. The modern scientific world-view to which their efforts gave birth presupposes a radical reshaping of our whole mental outlook. It involves a new approach to being, a new approach to nature, in short, a new philosophy. It is the main features of this philosophy that we now have to delineate.

First, however, an introductory remark should be made. For whatever else they may have been, these progenitors of modern science were not great thinkers. On the contrary, collectively they were instrumental in producing a body of thought representative of about the lowest level of intelligence to which the human mind has ever sunk. Hence although they were responsible for accomplishing what amounted to a philosophical revolution, they were not themselves philosophers, still less theologians, if these terms are meant to denote people whose mental powers are capable of grasping anything more than a handful of somewhat elementary concepts and ideas. To say that we have to delineate the main features of their philosophy does not mean, therefore, that we have to explore a complex, finely-wrought tapestry of wisdom—wisdom is about the last quality that distinguishes their system. We have only to try to bring into focus the few 'clear' and 'distinct' notions to which they gave single-minded adherence and which constituted the mainsprings of their activities.

The clue to the nature of these few uncomplicated notions that formed their philosophy is provided for us if we remember that whatever else they may not have been these men were brilliant mathematicians. I take it as axiomatic that if you do not have a true idea of what it means to be created in the image of God, you will inevitably create your 'God' in the image of whatever happens to be that characteristic in yourself, or in others, that you most admire or with which consequently you most identify. These men were no exceptions. They were themselves great mathematicians; and hence in default of any more profound understanding of things they identified their God with the great cosmic mathematician.

This may sound rather glib. But for them it was deadly serious—and the consequences for us are deadly serious. They were totally obsessed with this conviction, and interpreted it in the most literal, ruthless and uncompromising manner. God the mathematician was their Absolute, and to be coherent—to have logical meaning and hence reality—every deduction had to comply strictly with this initial and supreme dogma. As the cosmic mathematician, God makes the world through a mathematical system. God's mind is constituted of mathematical propositions, and it is by His immediate creative knowledge of His own mind that He thinks the world into existence in accordance with this pre-existing mathematical order. An infinite geometrical system is the real metaphysical background of the world of nature. This is to say that nature is fundamentally mathematical in structure, for mathematical laws and principles constitute the paradigm in accordance with which God created it.

This in effect means that mathematical principles are ultimately truths superior even to God, and independent of any divine revelation. In fact, in so far as divine revelation is significant at all, it is significant only so long as it is interpreted in a manner that does not contradict these principles. In themselves, these principles are truths of a transcendent kind. As such they do not belong properly either to philosophy or to theology, since they are the universal foundations and instruments of all the knowledge that human beings can acquire.

Mathematics is, then, the sole key necessary to unlock the secrets of nature, since the demonstrations of pure mathematics correspond to the objective truth of things, to the initial propositions of creation as they pre-exist in God's mind. It is the great mathematical system that is the substance of reality. The *a priori* assumption that the structure of the universe is mathematical means that physical reality is mathematical and that what is real in nature is only that which can be expressed in terms of strict mathematical laws. The real world is a world of mathematically measurable motions in time and space. If God created the world according to strict mathematical principles, it must follow that the whole realm of physics is reducible to mathematical qualities alone. And the corollary to this is that the only way in which it is possible for us to know objects in nature—to know natural phenomena—is through knowing their mathematical qualities, for it is these qualities alone that constitute their reality. What is ultimately real in nature is only that which can be expressed mathematically and of which mathematical knowledge is possible. Everything else—every non-mathematical quality—is irrelevant.

This, of course, immediately presented another kind of difficulty. The philosophizing of these pioneers of modern science was not carried out simply for its own sake. It was carried out for the purpose of unlocking the secrets of the world of nature, of giving us a knowledge of this world. This is the purpose that constitutes, ostensibly at least, the whole *raison d'être* of modern science: to explain the world we can experience through the senses, the sensible or sensory world. The scientist seeks to comprehend physical facts. But it is a consequence of the underlying assumptions of modern science that this comprehension, in so far as it is exact, must be expressed in mathematical language, because it is their mathematical qualities that constitute the reality of these facts. Thus any explanation with regard to physical facts can be true only if it is capable of expression in mathematical form. This means that the purpose of modern physics can be fulfilled only by reducing physical phenomena to mathematical formulae. Modern physics is the exact mathematical description of the bodies and motions of the physical world. It is the exact mathematical formulation of the processes of the physical world.

The world of physics is, then, the sensible world. But this world is uniquely characterized by qualities which are capable of having expression in mathematical formulae. Hence any explanation of it can be true only in so far as phenomena can be quantified. It is quantitative combinations that constitute the reality of the sensible world. It is the quantifiable elements of sense-fact that are its real constituents, and it is through the application of pure mathematics to these elements that we can deduce or demonstrate the reality of the sense-fact itself. Faced with a physical phenomenon, we must first therefore break it down or resolve it into its purely quantifiable elements—into the elements which it is possible to handle by the exact mathematical method—for it is these alone that are fundamental to its nature.

This at once puts in question the status of sense-objects, the objects we perceive through immediate sense-experience. It is clear that the assumption that the sensible world can be explained only in the language of mathematics must lead to explanations that do violence to immediate sense-experience. Indeed, Copernican astronomy itself is an early example of this—an example of mathematical logic violating one form of sense-experience and replacing it by another form. Sense-objects as we experience them through the senses are not therefore the real or mathematical objects—they do not constitute the real facts of nature. It is only certain aspects of them that are real, aspects like number, figure, magnitude, position, movement, which can be expressed mathematically.

Hence to discriminate between the real and the spurious—between what is a real fact of nature and what is not a real fact of nature—we have to apply the criterion of mathematics: the aspects of those things that can be perceived by the senses which are capable of being expressed in mathematical terms constitute the real fact of nature; what cannot be so expressed is not real fact but is illusory. Susceptibility to mathematical expression is the yardstick according to which we discriminate between what is true in nature and what is false. The senses themselves cannot discriminate: they mediate equally what is true and what is false. Sense-experience—what is called empirical experiment—is only relevant in so far as it relates to those characteristics in sense-objects that can be handled in the language of mathematics. Otherwise it is irrelevant. In fact all such experiment can do is to help decide between alternative deductions from clearly perceived first principles, and these principles are strictly and exclusively mathematical. The senses as such cannot perceive any object as it truly is, and sense-experience itself is not to be trusted.

This way of conceiving things imposed on the founding fathers of modern science a distinction that, apart from the premises of which it is the necessary logical resultant, appears so idiotic as to be non-sensical. None the less it was to become firmly embedded within the whole modern scientific system and crucial to its operation. This is the distinction between primary and secondary qualities. As we have seen, a central dogma of modern scientific thought is that only those qualities which it is possible to handle by the exact mathematical method are fundamental to nature, because only what can be expressed mathematically—what is quantifiable—constitutes the real object, the real fact of nature. This means, as we have also seen, that it is only qualities like number, figure, magnitude, position, and movement that constitute the reality of sense-objects, for only such qualities can be expressed in mathematical terms. It is these qualities that are described as primary qualities, and it is these qualities that alone actually inhere in sense-objects, because it is these qualities alone that furnish the possibility of mathematical handling.

This conclusion imposes the distinction in question. For in terms of our actual experience of sense-objects we do not by any means always apprehend in them only qualities that are susceptible to mathematical handling and can be expressed in mathematical formulae. We experience qualities—such as love, beauty, purpose, perfection, personality, soul, aspiration, and many others—that express value rather than quantity, and that elude the net of numbers. Yet according to the new scientific way of looking at things, such qualities cannot in fact inhere in sense-objects or constitute their reality, precisely because they are not quantifiable. Hence they must be radically distinguished from the qualities —the primary qualities—that do inhere in sense objects and do constitute the reality of these objects. And they are so distinguished by giving them the name of secondary qualities.

What must be emphasized is that all secondary qualities are said to be unreal—illusory—in so far as we attribute them to sense-objects or to the world of nature: nature as such knows nothing of such qualities and is entirely void of them. This means that in so far as we experience them in sense-objects it is because we ourselves project them on to these objects. They are actually entirely subjective, having no place in the realm of nature and no existence outside the individual human brain that experiences the illusion of their existence. Where the realm of nature is concerned, only primary qualities have any existence; it is they that are absolute, objective and mathematical, and that constitute the realm of knowledge, both divine and human. Secondary qualities are but relative, subjective, fluctuating and basically unreal, and constitute merely the realm of individual non-scientific opinion or pure illusion. They are totally irrelevant to truly scientific knowledge.

At this point a still more radical distinction is imposed. If secondary qualities are merely subjective modes of thought and as such have no place in the external, objective realm of nature, it must be that the realm of thought is a substance entirely different from that of the world of nature and exists entirely independently of the latter. Here we are at the root of that clear-cut, radical dualism between the world of thought and the world of sensible objects—between *res cogitans* and *res extensa* —chiefly associated with Descartes but endemic to and presupposed by the whole subsequent development of modern science and for all practical purposes still implicit in it.

The sensible world—the realm of nature—is independent of human thought to such an extent that it could operate as it does without human beings. Set over against it is an inner world whose essence is thinking and where everything is a mode of the thinking subject. This is the human mind (or the human soul, for the two terms have now become synonymous), the seat of the secondary qualities and confined by Descartes himself to an exceedingly meagre location within the human body. In according the mind (or soul) this pitiful position and status Descartes was reiterating his contemporary, Hobbes, who was already making an attempt to reduce everything, thought included, to bodies and mechanical motions, as well as to explain how secondary qualities are mere phantasmic unrealities which, although they appear outside us, are really caused by the clash of motions within us.

This view of the mind as something so entirely other than, and set over against, the realm of nature that there could be no real communion between them was, as I said, imposed on these pioneers of modern science because it was the only way of explaining what was for them axiomatic: that it is absolutely impossible for secondary qualities actually to be present in physical objects. Physical objects consist solely of primary qualities, those that can be expressed in the language of mathematics: this was unquestionable dogma and could brook no exception. Hence the non-quantifiable qualities that the mind might none the less attribute to physical objects cannot in fact have any existence in these objects; and the only way to ensure, conceptually speaking, that that must be the case is by positing the total independence of the mind from the world of sensible objects. Sensible objects are by definition mindless, soulless.

This, of course, put at risk the whole epistemological basis of modern scientific thought. If the mind is not and never can be in contact with the realm of nature and with physical objects, how can any certain knowledge of the latter be possible at all? How can the mind build up a coherent system of ideas that truly represent a world that is never accessible to it? How can we ever know in fact that there is such a world? Such questions, and others like them, could in the nature of things receive no plausible answer, for the simple reason that, given the underlying presuppositions informing the gestation, birth and development of modern science, there can be no plausible answer to them.

Instead, these questions are evaded by a specious form of circulatory argument. Since it is axiomatic, or an article of faith, that physical objects consist solely of primary qualities—qualities subject to the laws of mathematics—it follows that we can know such objects only in mathematical forms. Thus we can know, too, that the sole ideas occurring in the mind that can have any kind of objective reality in the sense that they truly apply to objects in the world of nature are mathematical ideas. That portion of the brain that is capable of mastering the laws of pure mathematics is the sole portion capable of giving us any true objective knowledge of the sensible world. All ideas other than mathematical ideas (except for a few logical propositions, such as that we exist, think, and so on) are purely subjective, mere unverifiable opinion when not simply total illusion.

This means that there is an insurmountable barrier between man and nature: man is man and nature is nature and never can the two really meet, far less interfuse. The world of nature is entirely under the reign of quantity: its total reality is quantitative, and can be expressed only in mathematical terms. Man cannot be expressed mathematically. Only what is superficial about him is susceptible to quantitative treatment. Otherwise he is largely a bundle of secondary qualities, subjective and hence unreal. The *real* world is *outside* man: the world of astronomy and of resting and moving objects, the world of primary qualities. Merely in that most abstract and impersonal part of his brain which can handle mathematics is there anything primary and real about him. It is with respect to this faculty alone that he can be said to be created in the image of God, and then only provided that in its workings it conforms and confines itself to mathematical rules. For the rest, man is simply an unimportant spectator and quasi-real object—an excrescence or appendage—of the great mathematical drama going on outside him; and if he can be said to have any purpose it is only in so far as he serves the aim of theoretical mechanics, only in so far as he is a devotee of mathematical science.

A mathematical view of nature inevitably involves a mechanical concept of its operations; and once man is seen as irrelevant where these operations are concerned, then what happens in nature must be thought of as happening according to mechanical necessity. Nature is merely a system of mechanical laws, a world of matter with no participation in any psychic or spiritual reality. It is true that for the pioneers of modern science God was credited with the initial creation of the world; but in practice it became increasingly, and eventually totally, assumed that after its first construction the world continued to exist quite independently of God. God was relegated to the first cause of motion, what happens in the universe after that being simply incidents in the regular revolutions of a great mathematical machine.

The world is not the body of God, and has no participation in Him. It is a great clock—material, not spiritual, mechanical, not teleological—which was once wound up by the Creator but now continues to function of its own accord in the mechanical manner in which it does function. If God has any part in this, it is simply to ensure that His arbitrarily imposed mechanical laws are not violated by irregularity. Yet it was not long before He was deprived even of this role: people like Laplace were showing that all irregularities are periodical and subject to an eternal law which prevents them from ever exceeding a certain stated amount; and the *coup de grâce* was administered by Kant, the overt purpose of whose analysis was to remove God from the realm of knowledge altogether.

With God eliminated from the scene, all that remained was to reduce the residual spirituality left locked up in the minds—or souls—of scattered human beings to mechanical products and to see them, too, as parts of the self-regulating cosmic clock. As we have noted, a start in this direction had already been made by Hobbes and Descartes; and what they had so well begun was consummated by scientifically-minded *philosophes* like La Mettrie in the eighteenth century and by the evolutionists of the nineteenth century.

With the human mind now appropriately slotted into it, the whole universe could be viewed as a vast despiritualized, mathematically computable system of masses moving in absolute space and time, hard, cold, colourless, silent, purposeless, impersonal and ultimately dead. As Dr Edward Caird, appointed Master of Balliol College, Oxford, in 1893, was so succinctly to express it in a book he published ten years before that:

> It is the peculiar strength of modern times that it has reached a clear perception of the finite world as finite; that in science it is positive, i.e. that it takes particular facts for no more than they are; that in practice it is unembarrassed by superstition, i.e. by the tendency to treat things and persons as mysteriously sacred. The first immediate awe and reverence which arose out of a confusion of the absolute and universal with the relative and particular, or, in simpler terms, the divine and the human, the ideal and the real, has passed away from the world.[3]

It would be hard to find words more apt to define the depths of disintegration and imbecility to which the modern mind has sunk.

These, then, are the main features of the paradigm of thought forged by the founding fathers of modern science between the sixteenth and eighteenth centuries; and it is this paradigm, shorn of its theological apparatus, non-Christian as it was, and with its totally inhuman conception of man at its heart, that passed into the general current first of European and then to an ever-increasing extent of world-wide public opinion. Its metaphysical presuppositions—having set in motion what rapidly grew into the over-riding, all-consuming and self-validated

3. Dr Edward Caird, *Hegel* (Edinburgh and London, 1883), p.112.

passion for subjecting the firmament to the dominion of mathematical mechanics, and so becoming unspecified, taken for granted and even forgotten—formed the settled background not only for further scientific thought but by and large for all other types of thought as well. In short, the world-view intrinsic to it became the dominant world-view of modern times.

Scientists—or some of them—may claim that today even physics has cut loose from its Cartesian and Newtonian moorings. Certainly this is true in many respects. Matter, for instance, is now conceived as a process or activity, not simply as solid particles moving in space, each particle being atomic and therefore physically indivisible and indestructible. In addition, to attempt to reconcile the conception of nature as a machine and the conception of all reality as permeated by process, as well as to give some meaning and purpose to this process itself, a theory of evolution, in various forms, has been invented—a theory, as I shall show in the next chapter, that is as superfluous as it is self-contradictory. In these and in other respects what is now known as 'classical' physics has been radically modified.

Yet though this is true, not only is it also true that a great deal of what is still regarded as valid scientific theory was produced under the aegis of 'classical' standards; but if evidence is needed of the degree to which the presuppositions of the paradigm we have been describing, especially the mathematical presuppositions central to it, are still dominant in shaping current scientific thought, it is amply provided in such a best-selling scientific work as Stephen Hawking's *A Brief History of Time*. As will be made more clear in the next chapter, the very notion that time has a history is itself unthinkable without the prior acceptance of a conception of time taken directly from the Galilean-Newtonian repertory of purely arbitrary hypotheses.[4] Moreover, modern physicists as a body certainly have not denounced this paradigm, including its mathematical basis, as representing the lie about things which it does not represent—not that modern Christian theologians have done much better.

In any case, this paradigm has certainly not lost its grip over the many millions of men and women who for all practical purposes are chiefly responsible for determining the dominant forms of life, thought, action, work, education, behaviour, art and of virtually everything else in today's world. And when this is taken into account, then the barbaric

4. Stephen W. Hawking, *A Brief History of Time* (Bantam Books, 1989).

character of so many of these forms, from our modern industrial cities, and the rank dereliction of so many human lives lived within them, down to our depradation and mutilation of the world of nature and to the ensuing ecological crisis, becomes not only explicable but wholly inevitable.

If we contrast the paradigm of thought which has produced this state of affairs with the Christian view outlined in the last chapter, it is clear that a radical reversal in the way of looking at things has taken place. Put in its simplest terms, this reversal amounts to an attempt to identify reality merely with the world accessible to the senses or at least with the mathematical patterns which the mind can discover in the forms of the physical world and behind them. Prompted partially by what they took to be the ancient Greek idea of a static ideal mathematical world mirrored in the physical world, the fathers of modern science moved away from the Christian understanding of life towards a kind of soulless materialism. They sought for a mathematical perfection and order both in and behind the world presented to us through the senses. It is an order whose coordinates are thought to be identical with what the mind can represent in mathematical terms.

These terms are thought to provide the link between the sensory world and its metaphysical basis, between organic nature and the ideal geometrical patterns that constitute its reality. Reality is regarded as a world of perfect formal and abstract relationships, mathematical in character: an impersonal structure associated with perfect numbers like the musical scale of Pythagoras. The pursuit of mathematical knowledge is regarded as the same thing as spiritual development. The attempt to know the mathematical structure of things is regarded as an attempt to discover the nature of reality itself.

What this means in effect is that the mortal-immortal ambiguity in the Christian consciousness, to which the idea of transcending death gives a dynamic creative tension, is now replaced by a mind-matter dualism of the most radical kind and by an attempt to establish an equilibrium and order in terms of a this-worldly existence and consequently to eliminate the paradoxical as well as the triumphant vision of life which in the Christian view is embodied, as we saw, in the symbol of the Cross. Whereas in the Christian view the activity of the Logos is thought to go so far as 'piercing even to the dividing asunder of soul and spirit',[5] and man is to 'hate his life in this world'[6] and 'must lose it'[7] as a condition of

5. Heb. 4:12.   6. John 12:25.   7. Matt. 17:25.

his entry into true life, now such discrimination is to be ignored. Man is merely a rational animal, a compound of animality and reason. The ascendancy of this view in the European consciousness was achieved by eroding the full significance of the Christian image of man as this has been understood in all its plenitude.

What we have called the great contradiction, the decisive either-or of life, is overlaid by the acceptance of a new image of man, and the door is opened for the materialistic philosophers, secular psychology, and the purely quantitative and quantifying human mind. In so far as the symbol of the Cross retains any vital allegiance, concentration on its spiritual meaning now gives place to an increasingly emotional and even sentimental attitude. The Crucifixion itself, symbol of the triumph over death in which the figure of the Logos made flesh is that of a crowned king who even on the Cross preserves all the living majesty of God, now becomes increasingly but a call to mourning and its message one of physical death. The figure of Christ on the Cross is now purely that of a man who has died in circumstances of extreme cruelty and pain.

The symbol is naturalized, brought down to the level of a natural event produced by the conditions of this world. The choice is now for a version of human purpose to be achieved on this side of death. For the Christian, the centre of life lies on the other side of death. The humanists and the scientific philosophers who emerged subsequent to the Renaissance increasingly shifted the centre of life to this side of death. They increasingly eliminated the mystery of death, and with it the true inner drama of human life. In other words, they increasingly eliminated the original significance of the Cross.

Yet in so doing they tacitly suppressed the Christian idea that the human image can be fulfilled only through the realization of its more-than-human potentialities, and that such realization requires assent to facts which are consequently of a supra-human nature. They tacitly suppressed the Christian affirmation that Life and Reality are inaccessible to mathematical categories, that the aspect of things accessible to such categories is but a superficial aspect, and that true knowledge demands a break-through into human consciousness of something that lies beyond any ideal of mathematical logic and harmony. Instead, they set the abstract mathematical mind up at the centre of life and made it the sole arbiter of the truth about man, nature and everything else.

In this way they replaced the mortal-immortal antithesis in the Christian consciousness, in which matter, whatever its distinction from

45

the spirit, is still regarded as pregnant with divine seed, by this radical mind-matter dualism in which nature is increasingly degraded to the status of being an object or reality totally external to and independent of both God and man, mere lifeless matter set over against the mind and virtually meaningless except in so far as it can be reduced to a set of mathematical or mechanical ideas; ideas that can if necessary be implemented in some mechanical or technological form in order to serve man's economic or other self-interest.

It is a paradox that the apostles of modern science, in eliminating the Christian sense of the significance of death, and in seeking to acquire a knowledge of the natural world in terms that presuppose this dualism of mind and matter, opened the way to a desecration of the natural world, including the human body, of the most vicious kind. At the same time, by setting out on a path of abstraction, they have fostered the desecration of human life as well. More and more have we lost contact with the inner sources of beauty and purpose; more and more have we been cast adrift on the surface of reality until at length, all significance gone and even the 'last illusion'—that of belief in our immortality—finally destroyed —'Peri l'inganno estremo,/ch'eterno io mi credei'—we confront with annihilating despair 'l infinita vanita del tutto'.[8] Scientific materialism or materialistic science, of which our own condition and that of our world are the legacy, has resulted in a fatuity and degradation of life which would appear to be without precedent in human history.

What is involved in this loss of a vision of reality that embraces the dimension of eternity and immortality, with the consequent limitation of the scope of human life to ideals thought to be capable of fulfilment in terms of our purely mortal existence, is of course a shift in the mode of consciousness to which we have been persuaded to give our allegiance. In the Introduction I spoke of two dominant modes of consciousness: the angelic or spiritual consciousness, which is our higher mode of consciousness and which is capable of perceiving and experiencing things as they are; and our ego-consciousness, which is our lower mode of consciousness and which can perceive only the outward and material aspect of things, or things divested of their informing reality and life; and the shift to which I have just referred consists in the progressive eclipse of our higher consciousness and our increasing allegiance and even subservience to the norms of our ego-consciousness.

8. See Giacomo Leopardi, 'A se stesso'.

46

In such circumstances we are compelled to turn outwards, towards the world of sensory objects, of things extended in time and space, the changing reflections of realities we can now no longer perceive or experience. We submit ourselves to what is material, to the exterior appearance of things, and make this the focus of our attention. In short, we close ourselves up within our own individual and mortal self as we exist in the materialized space-time world.

As a result, we are forced to regard ourselves as inevitably and inescapably in bondage to the materialized embodied form of existence in which we are involved. We commit a kind of apostasy, a denial of what is superior to ourselves. Created free in God, we seek to be free in our own selfhood, in our own egos. It is the sin of Adam, the sin of pride that rapidly turns to greed. Our goals are increasingly limited to those thought of as being capable of fulfilment on this side of death, our needs and characteristics are more and more regarded as merely mortal, to be measured in terms of the purely temporal and finite standards of this world, and to be identified increasingly with our material well-being in this world.

All this is the natural and inevitable consequence of our loss of spiritual vision. No longer able to realize our dependence on what surpasses ourselves, or to conceive of our destiny as being fulfilled in dimensions of life and reality that lie far beyond the finite, temporal and mortal limits of this world and our materialized existence within it, we now regard ourselves as independent and self-sufficient beings, constituting a law unto ourselves, and everything else as grist to our own mills. And having at our disposal only the material world, and realizing our power over it, we turn to that and use it, not as a means through which we can contemplate the Divinity, but as something we are entitled to exploit to satisfy the needs and greeds of our purely mundane selves.

A false self-image, as I said, breeds a false world-view, and together they breed our own nemesis and the nemesis of the world. There is no way of escaping this. Why and in what manner the paradigm of thought that has fostered modern science, as well as the industrial and technological inferno that it has produced, is a radical misrepresentation of things, will, I hope, become clearer in later chapters in this book. But here certain immediate observations are perhaps called for.

In the previous chapter, when speaking briefly of Plato's cosmology, we noted that Plato had taken over from the Pythagoreans the idea that the reality of things, and that which is natural to them, are features that can be described in mathematical terms; and that as it is their geometrical structure or form that can be so described, it is consequently this structure or form which determines in each particular case what a thing is and how it behaves. Once this idea is accepted as axiomatic, and you can think mathematically, you can develop a physics in which clear and certain knowledge of things is—or appears to be—more attainable than in any other way.

Of course, whether such knowledge is true or spurious will itself depend on the truth or falsehood of the axiom which it presupposes. In the present instance, the axiom in question is that the nature of things is determined by their geometrical structure or form, and that consequently not merely the shapes or patterns that things may assume or receive—their *apparent* reality—but also their particular properties or qualities—all that gives them true reality and life—can be expressed in mathematical terms.

It was basically, and in some ways explicitly, this Pythagorean-Platonic standpoint that the pioneers of modern physics were reasserting when—to use Galileo's terminology—they proclaimed that the book of nature is a book written by God in the language of mathematics, although the mathematics they had in mind were very different from those of the ancient Greek world. What they are presupposing is that the behaviour of natural things, and that by virtue of which they severally and collectively are what they are, is an effect of their mathematical structure. It is this structure which is thought to be the basis of qualitative differences and changes in nature, and hence these differences and changes are themselves regarded ultimately as quantitative and so as amenable to mathematical expression. The truth of nature is assumed to consist in mathematical facts: what is real in nature is what is measurable and quantitative, and this in geometric terms. In the end science becomes virtually synonymous with the analysis of such structure or form.

However, there are essential differences between the Pythagorean and Platonic standpoint and that of the seventeenth century physicists. First, the Pythagoreans and Plato conceived the world as a living organism, endowed with immanent energies and forces which are not only vital and psychical but also supranatural and spiritual in character; and it is these energies and forces—love and hate, reason and sense, pleasure and pain, aspiration and despair—that are regarded as the causes of natural processes. Moreover, in this Greek organic view of things, both formal and efficient causes are regarded as being not only *in* the world of nature, but also as transcending it.

This kind of animism was rapidly eroded from the minds of sixteenth and seventeenth century scientists by their increasing subservience to the mathematical principle; and even where traces of it were still present in the fifteenth and early sixteenth centuries it was not taken for granted, as in Greek thought, and the understanding that both formal and efficient causes are ultimately rooted in archetypal transcendent realities was already largely eclipsed. It was finally eliminated altogether when the idea that nature is an organism was replaced by the idea that nature is a machine. For the organic view presupposes either the identification of nature with God or their participatory reciprocity, while a machine presupposes either no God at all or a God that is totally outside it.

Yet whether any science, Pythagorean, Platonic or modern, that is based on the principle of mathematics can yield a knowledge not merely of the shapes and patterns that things in nature may assume or receive, but also of their intrinsic properties and qualities, depends, as we said, on the validity of the axiom it presupposes. It depends upon whether the reality of things in nature, that by virtue of which they are what they are and that which gives them life and being, can be expressed in mathematical terms. If it cannot be, then the so-called knowledge acquired as a result of assuming that it can be may tell us something about the shapes and patterns of things—about their apparent reality—as they seem to us; but it will not tell us anything about what things are in themselves and what constitutes their essence.

For if what things are in themselves and what constitutes their essence cannot be expressed in mathematical terms, this will mean that the geometric structure and form of things can tell us nothing about their intrinsic reality. Yet if that is the case, the kind of conclusions reached with regard to the nature of the physical world under the aegis of the paradigm of thought we have been describing in this chapter cannot constitute an integral science of nature; such conclusions cannot embrace the dimension of things that pertains to their reality and makes them what they are. They can only give us information about how things appear to us when we fail to perceive and experience this dimension of things—when we are, in other words, victims of an illusion.

For contrary to everything asserted in this paradigm, nature never affirms itself only in what can be measured and is quantifiable. It does not work out or exemplify mathematical qualities apart from qualities of life

49

and reality that are totally inaccessible to mathematical categories. It cannot be explained by what are numerical patterns and formulae, because it is not determined by geometric structure and form, and does not manifest merely what is evident in such structure and form. The reality or quality of anything in the natural world is not to be identified with its structure or its pattern, and nor is it to be explained by them.

On the contrary, there is a double aspect in everything to be found in nature. All natural forms and organisms are first of all functions, expressions or images of non-mathematical life and reality and enshrine the non-mathematical qualities that pertain to this life and reality: these qualities constitute their intrinsic nature and may be called their primary qualities. Then, second, they possess a limit, a shape, a pattern, qualities that are accessible to mathematical expression; and these qualities are purely exterior and may be called their secondary qualities.

These two aspects, the first of image-qualities and the second of pattern-qualities, are inseparable in every organism and form of nature, down to the most humble: every such organism and form is a bi-unit of life and pattern. But though inseparable, the two aspects are distinct: the image- or life-qualities are totally different from pattern-qualities. The pattern-qualities refer to the outer, inferior aspect of things, to what limits them. The image- or life-qualities give things their reality by linking them to Reality itself and by allowing them to partake of Reality itself.

Here, however, a further clarification should be made. For although the image- or life-qualities are totally different from the pattern-qualities, this does not in the least mean that they correspond to the psychic aspect of things while the pattern-qualities correspond to their material aspect. It is true that every material object has its counterparts in the soul, and may be said to symbolize with these counterparts. But such psychic counterparts are themselves subordinate, in that they derive their existence from a world that transcends the psychic as well as the physical domain altogether. This world is the spiritual or divine world, and it is this world that embraces the true archetypes or productive causes of all that appears in the psychic and physical domains, transmitting its qualities of life, being and consciousness to these latter domains but at the same time remaining utterly beyond them.

The significance of this will be explained more fully in the final chapter of this book. Here all that needs to be emphasized is that although every natural form and organism may participate in its transcendent spiritual archetype, and may be said to constitute an image of that archetype, the qualities—of life, being, consciousness and so on—of which it partakes by virtue of the fact that it is such an image, and by virtue of which it is that which it is, all pertain to the spiritual world and in their essence completely transcend the form or organism in which they are manifest.

This means that in themselves the two sets of qualities—the image-qualities and the pattern-qualities—are incommensurable and there is no logical connection between them: there is no way in which the image-qualities can be deduced from the pattern-qualities, and image-qualities do not in any way depend upon pattern-qualities. It is simply that in the bi-unit of an actual organism the image-qualities are given a form because of the presence of pattern-qualities. But these pattern-qualities have no subsistence of their own; they subsist only by virtue of the image-qualities that inform them; and it is the presence in them of these image-qualities that make them apparent realities.

There is a further consequence of what has just been said that should also be noted. I have already referred in this chapter to the crucial distinction between our ego-consciousness and our angelic or spiritual consciousness. This distinction has its immediate relevance in the present context, in that while our ego-consciousness can perceive only the outward aspect of things—their pattern-qualities—and is totally incapable of perceiving their image-qualities, our angelic or spiritual consciousness can perceive simultaneously in every organism and form the bi-unity of image- and pattern-qualities that constitutes its identity and reality. The spiritual consciousness, that is to say, sees things whole and sees them as they are, while the ego-consciousness can see them only in so far as its own opacity permits it to see them, which means in effect that it can perceive only those external aspects of them that are accessible to the senses, or their purely physical aspects. If it acknowledges anything more than the purely physical aspect of things, this is confined to the soul and to their psychic aspect, and this will then be regarded as the highest aspect of them that can be known. What was first affirmed in the Introduction to this book cannot be too often stressed, namely, that how we perceive something depends first of all on the mode of our consciousness or, to put this in another way, that nothing can be known except according to the mode of the knower.

This in its turn means that the image-qualities in things—their life, consciousness, being and all that gives them their reality—can never be objects of empirical observation in the modern scientific sense, and so can never be accessible to scientific analysis and investigation. For these qualities are presences of the Spirit, and by definition the Spirit is always subject and can never become object; while—again by definition—the ego-consciousness, which is the mode of consciousness effective for the modern scientist (for if it were not he would not be a modern scientist), is still in the thrall of a dualism between subject and object, knower and what is to be known, observer and what is to be observed, and hence cannot perceive anything that lies beyond the psycho-physical sphere. Like is known only by like. To know the Spirit you have to equate yourself with the Spirit. To know the nature of the image-qualities in things—these presences of the Spirit—you have to have regained the angelic or spiritual mode of consciousness. Indeed, it may even be said that until we do regain our spiritual mode of consciousness we are still subhuman, capable at best of perceiving merely the outward aspect of things, the husks of reality or what the Qur'ān calls the 'scum of illusion' (XIII: 17), but incapable of perceiving reality itself.

What has to be realized is that the modern scientific paradigm of thought completely inverts the natural order of things. In fact, it does more than invert it: it completely disrupts it. It not only attributes to what are secondary qualities—the pattern-qualities in things—a primary status. It also asserts that the true primary qualities in things, those that give them life, reality, personality, sacredness, soul, and which are inaccessible to mathematical expression, are not present in things at all, and that it is merely the impersonal, abstract pattern-qualities which can be expressed in mathematical terms that constitute their reality. In this way what are now regarded as sensible objects, natural organisms and forms, are these objects emasculated of their reality, of what gives them life and being, for their reality, life and being transcend the scope of mathematics. But mere pattern-qualities—mere mathematical qualities or qualities susceptible to mathematical expression—when divorced and abstracted from the image- and life-qualities from which in sensible objects themselves they are inseparable, become just so many ciphers, dead and unreal, but exposed on their own level to endless manipulation in total disregard and ignorance of the being and reality that they do in fact enshrine and manifest.

It is because this paradigm of thought predicates a view of nature that inverts and disrupts its intrinsic order, and leads to mistaking for natural objects what are only such objects emasculated of everything that gives them reality and life, that it is so fraught with consequences which themselves disrupt and pervert the natural world. For if you act towards nature in accordance with an understanding of nature that represents a total violation of its reality, you cannot expect what you do not to violate it also.

If we now ask how it is that such an inversion of things became embedded in the world-view that is still to all intents and purposes the dominant world-view of modern times, the answer is that it is implicit in the preliminary assumption from which this world-view itself derives. We have seen that the paradigm of thought which we have been describing is based on the notion that God is a cosmic mathematician. According to this notion God's mind is constituted of mathematical propositions, and it is by virtue of His immediate creative knowledge of His own mind that He thinks the world into existence in accordance with the pre-existing, immutable mathematical laws that characterize it. We further saw that the notion that God is essentially mathematical turns out to be the equivalent to assuming that mathematics is God. An infinite mathematical system becomes the real metaphysical background of the world of nature. Thus what is real in nature, and in man as part of nature, are only those aspects of both that express or reflect the mathematical paradigm and are consequently accessible to mathematical interpretation.

It is because mathematical principles come to be regarded in this way as truths ultimately superior to God that the notion that the fundamental structure of the world is mathematical could survive the elimination of God from the scene altogether. Yet this elimination did have the effect of depriving the exponents of the 'new philosophy' of the sole ground they possessed for claiming that their thought was rooted in objective reality—namely, the mind of God. But once God was eliminated from the scene the notion, unassailed and unchallenged, that an infinite mathematical system constitutes the real metaphysical background of the world of nature is rooted nowhere except in the pure subjectivity of the human minds that happen to give their assent to it. The original act of faith that saw God in mathematics and mathematics everywhere is now transferred to a purely secular idol, not to say to a fetish: it is transferred to the preliminary assumption that the objective truth of things is capable of being expressed in mathematical terms. But the fact is that this preliminary assumption of modern physics is now, metaphysically speaking, rooted nowhere: it is an entirely subjective notion, a psychological quirk of mere animal perception.

The pioneers of modern science and their successors are not of course wrong in thinking that objects in the natural world possess quantifiable aspects, aspects that can be expressed mathematically. But they are wrong in thinking that these aspects constitute what is important and real about such objects; and they are doubly wrong in thinking that what is important and real in them can be expressed in mathematical terms at all. What can be measured by mathematics is only the minimum in things. It is only what I called above the pattern-qualities in things. Such qualities are common to all things because without them the non-mathematical image-qualities in things—those that do constitute their reality—would have no exterior form, no shape or limit, and so would be totally in-accessible to all sense-perception. But what limits a thing, its exterior aspect, or what makes its reality apparent, is not the thing itself. If you start, therefore, with a point of view from which you choose those aspects of an indifferent nature which are quantifiable in order to form concepts of particular objects, you end up merely with abstract concepts—concepts that represent merely what is left of concrete objects when they are stripped of all that makes them alive and real.

This is the original sin in the thought of the pioneers of modern science, and it is still the original sin of contemporary physics in so far as it is dependent for its knowledge on the mathematical treatment of things. An adequate concept of a particular object or organism cannot start with such preliminary subjectivism in selecting the qualities that are then said to define what is true and knowable about it. Yet this is precisely the method by which modern physics, in so far as it is mathematical, proceeds. It selects as relevant to the concept of particular objects or organisms only those aspects of them that are common to all of them because by definition they have to be aspects that can be measured by mathematical procedures.

This is to say that particular objects or organisms have to be reduced to their lowest common denominators before they can enter into the conceptual world of modern mathematical science. It is these lowest common denominators—the minimum with which it is known that all instances comply—that provide the raw material of the concepts that this science works with and on. And it is these concepts, entirely abstract as they are, and arbitrary, that then pass as explanations or descriptions adequate to the realities of the sensible or sensory world.

If deductions from the preliminary assumption underpinning the subsequent explanations and demonstrations of modern mathematical science conclude in a view of nature that represents an inversion of its intrinsic order, this must be because the preliminary assumption itself represents a form of inversion. This assumption is originally a theological assumption. It is that the divine mind is subject to the laws of mathematics, or that ultimate Reality is a mathematical reality. It is because of this that relative reality—the world of nature—is also assumed to be mathematical.

The inversion, then, represented by this preliminary theological assumption must consist in elevating to the level of ultimate metaphysical Reality itself what is in actuality but one of its subordinate and inferior properties, a property that comes into play only in relation to the manifestation of Reality but which does not characterize Reality as such. It is the property that gives form and limitation to Reality, that shapes Reality into patterns and makes it apparent reality but that does not compose Reality itself and is other than Reality itself. As we shall see more clearly in the final chapter of this book, it is a property that pertains to what is itself a subordinate principle within Reality, a principle whose function is to mediate between ultimate metaphysical Being and the world of phenomena but that is also in itself other than this Being; that manifests the Absolute but is in itself purely relative.

It is, then, the elevation of what is in itself but the property of abstract patternness from the inferior rank of relativity to the superior rank of absoluteness that determines the inversion implicit at every level in the subsequent structure of that paradigm of thought which I have been describing; for what it amounts to is the degradation, to an inferior rank, of Reality itself, of Being itself, and even their exclusion from the scene altogether. So much so is this the case that the qualities of Reality and Being—of Life itself—present in every particular form or organism in the natural world, and constituting its reality and life, are now regarded as secondary qualities and even as mere subjective illusions, while primacy and reality are attributed to the qualities of abstract patternness alone. It is this that accounts for the grotesque yet devastating parody which passes for an understanding of man and nature in this paradigm; and it is this, too, that accounts ultimately for the crisis that we now confront. God does not write the book of nature in the language of mathematics, and it requires eyes informed by a knowledge quite other than that of mathematics in order to read it rightly.

3 The Apotheosis of Time and the Bogey of Evolution

IN THE PRECEDING chapter I made a statement to the effect that the theory of evolution, whatever the form it takes, is as superfluous as it is self-contradictory. Since this theory is so deeply entrenched within current scientific orthodoxy that it is scarcely too much to say that it underpins all modern scientific cosmological thought, to question its credibility is to question the credibility of this thought as a whole. That is why I feel that before going on to discuss the epistemological issue as such I should explain what I mean by describing evolutionary theory in this manner.

In order to do so with any effect, however, it is not only necessary to set this theory of evolution against the background of previous bodies of thought that account for the processes of temporal movement and change in ways quite other than those of evolution; it is also necessary to set it against the background of the scientific paradigm I have described in the previous chapter, for it is aspects of this paradigm that determine its essential character. This in its turn means that the first part of this chapter must be taken up with looking briefly at some of the main features of the cosmological doctrines of Plato, Aristotle and Christianity in so far as they relate to the matter in hand; for it was by and large these doctrines that dominated European cosmological thought at least until the time of the Renaissance.

As already noted in chapters one and two above, for Plato the structure or form which is 'in' natural things or human actions constitutes their essence. This essence may not be the pure form itself, but it is its imitation, and as such it is endowed with a tendency, or *nisus*, to aspire towards the realization of pure form. Thus each thing in nature—in the world of Becoming—possesses not only its transcendent, eternal and intelligible archetype, which accounts for its distinction from all other things; it possesses also its own immanent form, an imitation of its eternal form and having an affinity with it, which accounts for its growth, mutation and even transformation on the plane of its temporal existence.

The whole world of nature is thus a copy, however at times inexact, of its archetypal world of pure forms and is imbued with the aspiration towards the realization of the perfection and immortality of its archetypal world. This both explains why it undergoes perpetual change and gives an objective orientation and purpose to the process of change within it. In spite of lapses, the world of temporal becoming naturally aspires to the world of eternal Being. Or, to adapt Plato's phrase in the *Timaeus*, time and all things possessing a temporal aspect are moving images of eternity, eternity conceived not as mere timelessness but as a mode of being that transcends the kind of change that characterizes the world of Becoming and that involves no lapse because it perpetually fulfils its entire nature spontaneously.

Yet why should the world of nature depend for its existence, orientation and purpose on something that transcends it? Why can it not be regarded as existing of itself in its own right? Plato's answer in the *Timaeus*[1] is that the world of nature is a world of becoming or process, and that all becoming must have a cause. This does not mean that the facts presented to us by the natural world cannot be explained by showing what the relationship is between them or by explaining one of them in terms of the rest. But it does mean that as soon as we ask why facts that we call natural should exist at all, we are faced with a question that cannot be answered solely with reference to those facts themselves. The cause of phenomena cannot lie within the world of phenomena itself. It should be emphasized here that the word, 'cause', in Greek does not refer, as it tends to in modern scientific parlance, merely to an event prior in time to its effect; it applies to anything that provides a reason for the existence, appearance or determination of something else, without any temporal category necessarily being involved at all.

It might be said that in Aristotelian thought this Platonic view of the cause of the world of nature being an external cause is modified, and that

1. *Timaeus*, 28c.

for Aristotle the world is a self-causing and self-existing process, with no cause outside itself to account for the changes that take place within it. By definition the world of nature is for Aristotle a world of self-moving things. It is a world characterized by spontaneous movement, a world of process, growth, change. Because of this there is no need to posit a cause outside itself to account for the changes that take place within it.

Yet for Aristotle, these changes are not haphazard or random. They do not take place according to the law of chance. They constitute a development, a process directed towards a certain goal. As for Plato, things in the world of nature have teleological aspirations: they aspire to realize certain potentialities. But such potentialities, inherent as they may be in material objects, cannot be ascribed to matter as such. They must have immaterial causes, namely—to use Platonic terms—the forms specific to each particular thing that account for the way in which each grows and develops in order to realize the law of its nature.

Such immaterial, eternal forms, equally real and objective, are affirmed in Aristotle's thought, and exist in a transcendent state, apart from all matter, no less in his doctrine than in that of Plato. The difference in this respect between Plato and Aristotle is that whereas in the *Timaeus* God—the demiurge—fashions the world of nature upon the model of the archetypal immaterial forms of the intelligible world, in Aristotle's thought God, the single unmoved mover, is identified with these forms, which constitute a kind of plurality of unmoved movers, a complex of intelligences that, as in the *Timaeus*, form the immaterial and eternal model upon which the complex of movements and changes in the world of nature is modelled.

In both Plato's and Aristotle's thought, the differentiation of things in the world of nature, as well as the processes of change that they undergo, depend upon the logically, but not temporally, prior differentiation of their archetypes in eternal reality. It is because these archetypes represent so many intelligible modes in which God manifests His own self-contained activity—namely, His self-knowledge—and this activity is the highest and best possible, that they inspire the whole of nature with a desire or love (*eros*) for God and an aspiration towards Him, each thing fulfilling this aspiration in so far as it acts in accordance with its nature and with its own particular rank and capacity. This does not imply any theory of evolution in the modern sense; for the models according to which things in the world of nature develop from potentiality to actuality not only transcend this world but also form an eternal repertory, each related to the other not in any temporal sense but solely in terms of simultaneous dynamic reciprocity. The movement therefore through which each thing grows and develops in order to realize the law of its nature is not one of evolution; on the contrary, it represents the process of mutual exfoliation and infoliation that takes place between each thing and its eternal archetype.

Very much this same cosmological paradigm is effective in the pre-Renaissance European world, modified though it may have been by the overriding theological and philosophical principles of the Christian religion. Essentially it is the Aristotelian paradigm, the processes of change and mutation in the natural world being accounted for in much the same teleological manner as they are in Aristotle's thought. Implicit in all things in the world of nature is an aspiration towards the realization of the transcendent and immaterial world of pure Being, and it is this aspiration that lies at the basis of the processes of change and development that take place in this world. God is the One who eternally is and who continually draws into movement by His perfect beauty all that is potentially the bearer of a higher state of being. He is the divine harmony at the heart of all things, realized in His transcendent self-fulfilling activity, eternally present, Himself unmoved, yet the mover of all change. Hence ultimately all change and movement in the universe are inspired by love for God, 'the love that moves the sun and the other stars', as Dante affirms at the close of his *Divina Commedia*.

That the realization by each thing of its own intrinsic nature is so often frustrated, and its movement towards God deflected, is of course in the Christian world not ascribed, as it is in Platonic and Aristotelian thought, to the recalcitrance of matter or to the inability of natural forms totally to embody the pure forms of the intelligible world; it is ascribed, as we noted in chapter one, to the defection of the human will typologically figured in the fall of Adam from paradise, a defection which has exposed human beings to the influences, of a demonic kind, that persuade them to think and act in ways which, far from being in accordance with human nature, are radically at odds with it and destructive of it. And this vulnerability and self-alienation on man's part have introduced into the rest of the natural world an element of discord that frustrates and deflects what would otherwise be the ordered and rhythmical process through which all things move from imperfection to perfection, from potentiality to actuality.

It was this teleological understanding of the process of change and development in the natural world—the vision of nature as permeated by aspiration to realize or imitate eternal and immaterial forms present in it as latent possibilities—that was singled out for special attack by the sixteenth and seventeenth century pioneers of modern science. In its place they succeeded in establishing a new theory of nature and of change and movement in nature. According to this theory, all such change and movement are to be explained solely by reference to the action of already existing material things. It is the action of one such material thing, or of several such material things, that generates motion in other things, and thus produces the various types of structure found in the natural world.

In this view change is seen no longer as an expression of aspiration towards a transcendent and immortal state of being; it is seen simply as a function of mathematical structure. For the study of the *why* of motion is substituted the analysis of the *how* of motion, and this analysis is pursued by the method of exact mathematics. But the mathematical analysis of the *how* of motion inevitably involves regarding space as something purely geometrical and time as essentially mathematical; for to treat any motion mathematically is to analyse it into certain units of distance covered by certain units of time. And this in its turn means that space and time are thought to be fundamental objective categories, and the real world to be a world of material bodies moving in this space and time. [2]

Given that this new view of things, especially where the conception of time is concerned, was to produce such a deadlock in human consciousness that the only way out of it appeared to be the invention of the doctrine of evolution which is the theme of this chapter, it is pertinent perhaps briefly to examine more closely what is involved in it, even if it means repeating in this context certain things already stated in the preceding chapters. Centrally what characterizes the revolution in thought accomplished by the pioneers of modern science is no less than a total rejection of the teleological and spiritual conception of nature, that conception which lies at the heart of the Platonic-Aristotelian-Christian view of things that we have been describing.

In this view, the universe is a hierarchy of levels of being or of forms leading up to God or Pure Form. God is thus the final cause of all things just as truly as and even more significantly than He is their original Creator. Not only does everything in existence exist because it is a

---

2. For this new conception of time, and for its immediate consequences, see E. A. Burtt, *The Metaphysical Foundations of Modern Science*, op. cit., pp. 91 ff.

manifestation of a divine virtuality—a virtuality that constitutes its spiritual essence and identity; but also everything in existence only realizes its true destiny and nature on condition that it lives in harmony with its spiritual essence and identity. This means that it must actualize in itself the divine virtuality of which it is the manifestation. The final end of everything—its ultimate purpose—is achieved when it has realized its divine potentiality and has re-established itself in God.

Causality, therefore, has nothing to do with what we now call physical causality. In the nature of things, no visible, material phenomena can ever be the cause of other such phenomena. An immaterial cause is always required. The agent of temporal change and movement is the invisible, the immaterial, and its mode of acting is trans-temporal, although its effects are manifest in the temporal world. This is because the reality of any phenomenon resides in its symbiosis with what is non-manifest, trans-temporal and trans-spatial. There is no opposition or radical difference between the sensible and the intelligible, the physical form and the spiritual form, the finite and the infinite. On the contrary, there is intimate correspondence between the physical and spiritual, the finite and the infinite: one and the same being exists simultaneously on both planes.

Hence it is impossible to understand or explain the physical form of anything with categories of interpretation that pertain solely to the physical plane. The physical form of anything can be understood or explained only through a prior understanding of the qualities of the spiritual reality of which it is the physical form. Correspondingly, what happens on the visible, temporal plane is not determined simply by a preceding combination of events in the physical world, and cannot consequently be accounted for by reference solely to the physical world. Indeed, to attempt to account for what happens in nature in this manner is to presuppose that the physical world possesses an autonomous status as a finite reality. This in its turn involves attributing to the world of nature a status it does not possess, and investing it with a fictitious identity, which means that theories relating to this world based on such a misapprehension of its reality must also be fictitious.

Nature is, thus, fundamentally qualitative, consisting of things that collectively and severally are defined by the purpose for which they are created. The categories in terms of which these things are understood and interpreted, therefore, are those not of time, space, mass, energy and so on, but of substance, essence, matter, form, colour, sound, beauty, fragrance, receptivity to love, to joy, to compassion—qualities that are immediately present and fully intelligible *in the things themselves.*

Of this world of nature man is an integral part. Indeed, his place in it is fundamental, for he is in every sense the centre of the universe. Not only is he a genuine microcosm, exemplifying in himself the union of all things in the macrocosm; but also he possesses an essential intermediate and mediating role between God and the world He has created. He is thus a crucial link in the process of transformation through which things are led up the scale of being to their final resting-place in God.

It is this teleological process through which things are brought from a state of potentiality to a state of actuality, and in which man plays such a central part, that accounts for what we call temporal change. Such change is really a series of continuous transformations, involving all things, through which this process leading from potentiality to actuality is being accomplished. In it time is a very unimportant and insignificant factor. It is but the accidental epiphenomenon of qualitative substances, not in the least a fundamental category in its own right.

This teleological and spiritual conception of nature, and of man as the keystone of nature, is, as we said, totally rejected by the pioneers of modern science. In fact, the thought-revolution which they accomplished is characterized by the substitution of a new mathematical science for the teleological physics we have just been describing. This of course involves the explicit denial that the kind of causality effective in the Platonic-Aristotelian-Christian view of things constitutes a valid principle of explanation. It is replaced by the notion that the cause of the observed facts of nature—the reason why they are what they are—is the underlying mathematical harmony discoverable in them.

A corollary to this is the notion that what constitutes the real objects in nature are not the non-quantifiable qualities with which they are identified according to the spiritual conception of nature. What constitutes them are merely the qualities that can be expressed mathematically—qualities such as number, figure, magnitude, position, motion. These are the real and primary qualities. All the other and non-quantifiable qualities are secondary, subjective and irrelevant to the constitution of true objects.

This new attitude applied not only to objects in nature but also to the relations between them: these, too, were said to be fundamentally mathematical. Physical space comes to be thought of as identical with the realm of geometry, and to physical motion is attributed the character of a pure mathematical concept. The real world is the world of bodies in mathematically reducible motions, and this means that the real world is a world of bodies moving in time and space—a world of mathematically measurable movements in time and space.

In place of the teleological categories in terms of which change and movement are interpreted according to the spiritual conception of nature are now insinuated the two essentially insignificant and accidental categories of time and space. But to interpret temporal processes in these terms means giving time and space quite a new status. It means attributing to them new meanings as mathematical continua and elevating each of them in its own right to the rank of an ultimate metaphysical principle, independent of the material bodies that occupy it. The processes of change and movement are no longer to be understood as a series of continuous transformations whereby things pass from potentiality to actuality; they are to be understood as events taking place in a mathematically measurable duration. But this notion that the temporality of motion is reducible to the terms of exact mathematics means that time becomes an irreversible fourth dimension. It is absolute, infinite, homogeneous, continuous, independent of any sensible object, and flowing —in a way that can be represented by a straight line—uninterruptedly and equally from eternity to eternity.

What one is witnessing is a veritable apotheosis of time. One might say that in the modern scientific secular consciousness time assumes the status possessed by eternity in the spiritual consciousness. Viewed thus, such an idolization of time corresponds precisely to the degree to which the sense of eternity has been eroded. This process has not only made possible the production of such fantasies as H. G. Wells's *The Time Machine* but has attained its apogee in the notion, exemplified in the title of the book, *A Brief History of Time*, by Stephen Hawking mentioned in the last chapter, that time itself has a history. As this new status accorded to time is, like the autonomous status accorded to the world of nature, a purely fictitious status, it follows that any scientific theory which presupposes it is likewise fictitious.

This apotheosis of time involves a radically new view of the universe. First of all, the whole understanding of time as something lived in is at once eradicated. For if time is a measurable continuum it is no more than a moving mathematical limit between the past and the future. It is but a dividing line between the infinite stretches of a past that is irrevocably dead and the equally infinite stretches of a future that is forever unborn.

There is nothing actual. Even the present moment itself possesses no temporal quality. It is merely the moving limit in a process that issues from the past and into the future with an impersonal, indifferent and infinitely monotonous regularity.

Second, this notion of time as a measurable continuum presenting a moving mathematical limit between past and future means that we as human beings are effectively excluded from it. For the notion of time as a mathematical continuum makes it obligatory to think of causality solely in terms of forces revealing themselves in the mathematically expressible motions of matter itself. In fact, both causes and effects are now regarded as motions· and once this is assumed the stage is set for proclaiming the world to be a vast self-contained mathematical machine consisting of motions of matter in space and time. And in a world regarded as a perfect machine there is little or no place for man.

Assuredly, this expulsion of man from the world of nature was already more than implicit in the doctrine of primary and secondary qualities which became axiomatic for these pioneers of modern science. We have noted that in the Platonic-Aristotelian-Christian view man and nature are seen as sharing the same destiny, both involved in a divine-human drama whose consummation lies in the transformation and deification of all created being. But although sharing the same destiny, man's part in the drama in which both man and nature are involved is pre-eminent and crucial. He is nature's crowning glory and in every sense her integrating and principal protagonist. Whatever distinctions might be made between primary and secondary, being and non-being, man is allied consistently with what is primary and as such with what is most positive and creative.

The scientific thought-revolution we have been describing reversed all this. For with the new dogma of primary and secondary qualities erected by its perpetrators man is ousted from the real and primary realm. As we have seen, primary qualities are now identified exclusively with those features of sensible objects that are accessible to exact mathematical handling. It is these features alone that are now regarded as constituting the reality of such objects, as making them what they are and as giving them their identity. All non-quantifiable features they may or may not appear to possess—features that in the spiritual view of things are precisely those that constitute their reality and make them what they are—are now classed as secondary. As such they are subjective, unreal and ignoble, and totally irrelevant to the understanding of the vast mathematical system whose regular motions in time and space constitute the real world of nature.

Man is ill-accommodated to exact mathematical handling. His purposes, feelings, loves, strivings and practically everything else that characterizes his being and makes him what he is, are all non-quantifiable qualities. As such they are now regarded as secondary qualities, basically unreal and entirely alien to the real world of nature. It is this world of nature outside man—the world of astronomy and resting and moving terrestrial objects—that is now regarded as exclusively primary. As such it alone possesses true reality, is entirely pre-eminent and substantial, and it alone may be said to have independent existence.

Man has no part in this world. Except with respect to very minor features of his being, he is totally separated and cut off from nature, his soul holed-up in the obscurity of the darkroom which occupies a minute portion of extension within his brain. We are in the world of Cartesian dualism: on the one side there is the primary mathematical realm; on the other, the secondary realm, the world of man, a petty irrelevant onlooker of the great mathematical system which is the substance of reality and whose action goes on outside him, quite indifferent as to whether he is present or not present.

With all man's human qualities thus banished from the primary realm and his consequent elimination from the 'real' world of nature—identified now with material atoms in their mathematical relations—there is no place for final causality whatsoever. God—in so far as He is still regarded as having any role at all—is now reduced to being no more than the Efficient Cause of this system, the global mathematical inventor necessary to account for the first appearance of the atoms but thereafter with no part to play. Thus He, too, to all intents and purposes is effectively banished from the cosmic process.

With God's exit from the scene, there is no longer any goal or purpose in the processes of change that take place. The 'real' world—the world of nature—is simply a succession of atomic motions in which one moving object impels another *ad infinitum* with mathematical regularity through the vast continua of time and space, blind, purposeless, impersonal, pitiless and deprived of all significance and meaning. And of this world man is the chance, fleeting and ultimately superfluous by-product. Such is the world-view—which must surely rank as one of the most benighted and inhuman ever to have issued from the human mind—that has become the predominant world-view of modern times.

It is also this world-view that has imposed on the nineteenth century and subsequent descendants of the fathers of modern science the need to invent the doctrine of evolution. And it is to the question of why this is the case that we must now turn our attention.

As we have seen, the real world is identified by the fathers of modern science with material atoms in their mathematical relations. But with the elimination of the understanding that God is the ultimate active agent of all temporal events and changes, responsibility for what occurs in this world could be intelligibly attributed only to the motions of the atoms themselves. Everything that takes place in this world is the effect solely of mathematical changes in these basic material elements. Causality is increasingly lodged in the atoms themselves. But neither this causality nor what it produces has any purpose or meaning. The whole world-process is blind and pointless. And it is here that lies the motive for the invention of the doctrine of evolution.

That this is the case is due initially to certain inherent characteristics of the human intelligence. For knowledge of the meaning and purpose of things, including itself, is built into the human intelligence as the very essence of its nature. Thus the more the intelligence becomes aware of itself, the more it perceives this meaning and purpose; and, conversely, the greater its degree of self-ignorance, the more things will appear to it to be meaningless and without purpose. The rider to this is that it will perceive things as meaningless and without purpose only so long as it is content to frustrate its own nature, while, correspondingly, the first sign of its becoming aware of itself will be evident in its attempt, however tentative and erratic, to descry meaning and purpose.

From this point of view the failure on the part of the pioneers of modern science to place teleological issues at the heart of their explana-tions, and their radical exclusion of such considerations, represent the virtual elimination of the human intelligence from the scene of scientific enquiry; and the inevitable consequence of this elimination was the notion that the processes of nature are ultimately meaningless and without purpose.

The way through which the human intelligence recovers its intrinsic knowledge of the meaning and purpose of things, including itself, is one whereby it returns to itself, overcoming its self-estrangement. It is one of self-recollection. Given the degree to which this intelligence had been eclipsed where the doctrines of the pioneers of modern science are concerned, this process of recovery could not be other than a slow one. One of the forms, perhaps the main form, in which it was initially expressed is the theory of evolution, the attempt to restore a sense of purpose and meaning to the succession of events that take place in what is conceived to be the endless flow of time.

A perfectly cogent and coherent explanation for these events, whether related to the origin of the species or to the so-called fossil record, is of course to be found in the Platonic-Aristotelian-Christian cosmology,[3] without there being any need to invent a new theory. I say 'of course' because this cosmology, being the expression of man's higher or spiritual consciousness and therefore based on a perception and experience of things as they are in reality, cannot but provide explanations adequate to all that takes place in the world of phenomena, however much there may be variations of nuance and emphasis in the different forms it is given by its individual interpreters. This latter comment applies not only to the different forms it takes in the western world, but also to those it takes in the major metaphysical doctrines of other civilizations, of which an example would be the Vedanta doctrine of the Indian world.

Such doctrines, however, were excluded *a priori* from the repertory of nineteenth century and later scientists, even had they been aware of them. For however imperative it became for them to try to restore some meaning and purpose to the mechanical model of the universe bequeathed to them by the fathers of modern science, they did not on that account challenge any of the main dogmas according to which this model was itself constructed. On the contrary, they accepted them as axiomatic and indisputable. And, as we have seen, these dogmas explicitly presuppose the rejection of the Platonic-Aristotelian-Christian view *in toto*. Yet why should this mean that the attempt to restore this meaning and purpose should take the form of a theory of evolution?

The answer to this is that these dogmas or presuppositions, unquestioningly accepted as they were, made the adoption of such a theory inevitable. First, the loss of consciousness of the world of eternal archetypes, of which the physical appearance of things is the spatial and temporal extension, meant that it was no longer possible to relate directly temporal events and phenomena to their trans-temporal sources. This in

---

3. For an interpretation of the fossil record in the light of this cosmology, see, for instance, the article by Michael Negus, 'Man, Creation and the Fossil Record', in *Studies in Comparative Religion*, Winter 1969, pp.49–55.

its turn meant that the occurence of such events and phenomena could be accounted for only by saying that they are produced by other temporal events and phenomena which had occured before them.

This in its turn presupposes the conception of time which we have been describing: that time is a fundamental metaphysical category, absolute, infinite, independent of sensible objects, and flowing uninterruptedly from eternity to eternity. It is within this vast continuum that events and phenomena are thought to succeed one another in interminable succession, those antecedent in this continuum producing those that occur subsequently. And in so far as there is any positive causality in the events and changes that take place within this continuum, this is lodged in their basic material elements, the atoms.

Thus to give some meaning and purpose to this whole process could be done only by attributing them in some way to the events and changes that occur in what is conceived to be a purely linear and irreversible time-dimension. Instead of these events and changes being regarded as haphazard and arbitrary, they had to be invested with an internal logic. The causality lodged in the atoms themselves had to be presented as operating according to some intelligible principle or principles. Things had to be seen as moving from the past into the future in obedience to a coherent pattern. And it is the attribution of coherent pattern to the movement of things from the past and into the future that constitutes the essence of what comes to be known as evolution.

Given, then, the presuppositional framework to which the search to restore meaning and purpose to the processes of change and movement in the universe had to accommodate itself, it was inevitable that it issued in the theory of evolution. There is no other theory in which it could possibly have issued without violating the presuppositions of the framework itself; and such was the prestige accorded to their inventors, from Copernicus to Newton, that these presuppositions were accepted as axiomatic and unquestionable. And this applied above all to the conception of time.

This search for meaning and purpose represents, we said, an attempt on the part of the human intelligence, so eclipsed in the speculations of the founding fathers of modern science, to recover an awareness of its own intrinsic nature. Or one can put this another way and say that it represents an attempt to emerge from the mutilated and distorted view of the ego-consciousness in order to recover the integrity of a spiritual conception of the universe; or, in more direct terms, to break through the

machine model of the universe and to re-introduce into the understanding of things something of the teleological perspective that characterizes
the view of the higher non-materialized consciousness. So long as
physicists were content with their notion of a purely dead and mechanical
world of matter, they could not accept or even construct a theory of
evolution: such a world cannot possibly produce life by doing the only
thing it is capable of doing, namely, distribute itself in space. But once the
notion of life was introduced into the system, it was inescapable, for
reasons we have been examining, that the attempt to give meaning and
purpose to the processes of change in nature should take the form of a
theory of evolution.

This is why the first phase in the development of the concept of
evolution was biological, for it was the biologists who modified the
Cartesian dualism of mind and matter by introducing this notion of life as
a third principle mediating between them. Of course, this splitting up of
mind, matter and life into distinct realms itself represents another
aberration forced on sixteenth and seventeenth century scientists by the
logic of their presuppositions. By excluding the soul from their perspective, they could conceive the orderly movements of matter only as dead
movements, and Descartes himself could even think that it might be
possible to explain biological facts in terms of mechanical physics.

By the end of the eighteenth century, however, geologists were
beginning to form a picture of the past which appeared to disrupt the
currently accepted assumption that nature tended to reproduce fixed
specific forms of life; for according to this picture it was now becoming
clear that present-day flora and fauna were very different from what they
had been in the past. Nature must therefore be capable of producing new
and better forms—better in the sense that they are more fitted to survive
and live, or that they represent the idea of life more adequately.

Yet since everything that happens in nature is now regarded as
happening as a result solely of antecedent changes in the material
elements located in the dimension of time, what this new geological
picture was taken to postulate was that in order to produce organisms not
identical with themselves, specific forms of life must undergo changes in
time as the history of the world proceeds. Thus the whole process is
conceived by biologists as an endless succession of experiments on the
part of nature to produce organisms that embody more effectively and
intensely the principle of life.

Such a conception by no means yet signifies that this life is thought of as endowed with conscious purpose. Darwin speaks of natural selection, and his language is loaded with teleological implications where organic nature is concerned. But this process of natural selection (Darwin himself does not call it evolution) is still regarded as a blind process; nature is not a conscious agent pursuing goals consciously perceived.

None the less, this conception did prepare for the next phase of evolutionary theory, the cosmological phase. In this phase not only the development of a natural species or order is represented as a development in time, but also the development of the human consciousness itself is represented in the same way. In fact the whole universe is taken to be subject to the evolutionary process. Moreover, the process itself is no longer seen as merely a matter of blind chance. For if life, like mind, is conceived as developing itself through such a historical process, orientating itself in a determinate direction, and producing as it goes along organisms more fitted to survive in a given environment, then it becomes increasingly difficult to describe this process as a random process. Such a view of things clearly clashes head-on with the theory that modifications in specific forms depend on pure chance, which means that it also clashes with the materialist idea that physiological function can be explained wholly in terms of physico-chemical structure. In other words, it denies the validity of the conception of the world as a machine.

Yet here precisely lies the fatal incapacity of all evolutionary theory, whatever form it takes, ever to provide an explanation of things adequate to the intrinsic nature of the human intelligence, an explanation, that is to say, which corresponds to the vision of man's higher or angelic consciousness. For, as we have seen, the mechanistic view of the universe was itself imposed on the thought of seventeenth century scientists by their prior assumption that everything that happens is the effect solely of what has already happened: the real world is simply a succession of atomic motions in mathematical continuity. But this conception itself depends, as we have also seen, on another prior assumption, namely, that time, like space, is an ultimate metaphysical principle, a fundamental self-subsistent entity in its own right, absolute, infinite, independent of any sensible object, and constituting a kind of irreversible fourth dimension. It was this notion of time that made it possible, indeed inevitable, to explain causality solely in terms of forces revealing themselves in the mathematically expressible motions of matter itself, and hence to conceive the world as a machine.

It might be thought ironic that evolutionists should attempt to replace the machine model of the universe with something more living, purposeful and human, and yet accept as an ultimate *datum* precisely the notion of time that had given rise to the machine model in the first place. But such irony is inescapable once that notion of time is accepted; and, as we have seen, it was precisely its acceptance that conditioned the theory of evolution: given that notion, no other theory was possible. And this is still the case even though the idea that time and space constitute two entities has been replaced by the idea that they constitute but a single entity. For though this means that the idea that there is one infinite plurality of points and another of instants gives way to the idea that there is only a single infinite plurality of point-instants, everything that exists still has both a place-aspect and a time-aspect. In its place-aspect it has a determinate situation, in its time-aspect it is always moving into a new situation. All things are inherently possessed of motion, and all movements take place relative to each other within what is conceived as the vast space-time continuum as a whole.

Thus whether it is Darwin with his theory of natural selection; or Bergson with his conception of a life-force flowing in obedience to its own *élan vital* out of an infinite past onwards into an infinite future; or Lloyd Morgan with his theory of higher orders of being emerging from a single cosmic process that goes on endlessly and irreversibly; or Teilhard de Chardin, whose main ideas are reviewed in detail in a later chapter in this book; or, more recently, Rupert Sheldrake,[4] whose hypothesis of formative causation depends upon the assumption that things are as they are because they have been as they have been: all take for granted, and even as axiomatic, the conception of time which is basically that proposed—albeit as a pure assumption and in a manner entirely beyond the reach of any scientific experimental verification—by the seventeenth century pioneers of modern science.

A corollary depending from what has just been said must also be clear: remove this conception of time and you remove the basis on which the whole theory of evolution rests. You remove in fact the linchpin of modern scientific cosmology. Modern scientists themselves have not yet succeeded in doing this, though they have prepared the ground for doing so. For this conception of time in the thought of the pioneers of modern science itself presupposed another condition: that God had set the whole cosmic process in motion. Although God was no longer regarded as the

4. See Lloyd Morgan, *Emergent Evolution* (1923), and Rupert Sheldrake, *The Presence of the Past* (London, 1989).

71

Final Cause of things, He was still regarded as the first Efficient Cause, even if He was thought not to be the formal agent of everything that takes place once He has set things in motion.

Thus this conception of time as a fundamental metaphysical category was regarded, however mistakenly, as rooted in ultimate Reality itself, in God Himself. But once God is eliminated from the scene, it is rooted nowhere except in the pure subjectivity of the mind that happens to give credence to it. Apart from this, it simply dangles in a meaningless metaphysical void, as arbitrary and whimsical as it is beyond any conceivable verification. That is why the theory of evolution, which presupposes this conception of time, itself ultimately dangles in a meaningless metaphysical void. And this signifies that it is incapable of responding to the intrinsic nature of the human intelligence: it cannot by definition do what it sets out to do, and that is to provide an understanding of the meaning and purpose of things that is more than mere arbitrary and purely subjective hypothesis. A theory that itself dangles in a meaningless metaphysical void cannot possibly give meaning to anything.

If further evidence of the inability of the theory of evolution to provide a meaningful explanation of things is required, it can be found in the essentially self-contradictory character of the theory itself. One feature endemic to it is enough to demonstrate this. According to this theory the whole universe, including man's mind or consciousness, is evolutionary. This being the case, then evolution must constitute a universal and eternal law governing all the processes that take place within the space-time continuum.

Yet if the human consciousness is itself still in the process of evolving, then it cannot possess *in toto* the capacity to know the truth. In fact, as Bergson pointed out, it cannot be a truth-knowing faculty at all. How, then, or by virtue of what, does it suddenly emancipate itself from the whole process of evolution to which it is subject, stand outside this process, and perceive and formulate an eternal truth said to apply to the process itself?

It could do this only on condition, first, that there is an eternal realm of ultimate metaphysical truths, transcendent to the space-time world itself; and, second, that it has reached a point of evolution at which it is capable of grasping these truths. This is tantamount to saying that it must have attained the fullest degree of consciousness of which it is capable, and cannot evolve any further; for it would be absurd to say that human consciousness can evolve beyond the point at which it can perceive and grasp ultimate metaphysical truths.

So far as I am aware no evolutionist has so far postulated that human consciousness has reached its ultimate point of development. But unless it has done this it possesses no capacity whatsoever to pronounce on the nature of eternal metaphysical principles. It has no title even to affirm that there are such principles, much less to affirm that there is a universal law to which all things in space-time are subject. To make such affirmations you have to know the truth, and by definition the human mind still in the process of evolving cannot be a truth-knowing faculty.

Moreover, if the human consciousness still in the process of evolving can at one point in time escape from the evolutionary process in order to grasp an eternal law governing the process, why not at another point? But in that case anyone on the basis merely of his own *ipse dixit* could claim to have grasped such an eternal law. And in such circumstances, according to what criteria is it possible to distinguish between a genuine expression of a fundamental metaphysical principle and what is merely the expression of a purely subjective, whimsical and individual conception of things?

The fact is that the theory of evolution negates its own validity simply in asserting what it does assert. For a theory which announces that the human consciousness is still evolving simultaneously announces that the consciousness still immersed in the process of evolving cannot know the truth about anything. In fact, if everything is in a state of evolution, on what basis can a valid statement be made about anything?

Why a theory that would appear to demand such a singular lack of respect for the integrity and coherence of the human intelligence should capture the allegiance of so many minds might seem something of a puzzle. Yet if for the moment one can reduce things to the individual psychological plane, one can see that it is a theory extremely flattering to the ego-centred human psyche. For it fosters the illusion that we have not only the capacity but also the obligation to produce new theories of reality. We have the capacity because, if the human consciousness evolves through the linear time-dimension, the consciousness that stands, as any contemporary living consciousness must stand, at the most advanced point in time between past and future is, or can be, superior, if only fractionally, to any consciousness that has come before it. It is therefore capable of perceiving and formulating a more adequate conception of reality than any of its predecessors.

A rider to this is of course that past theories about the nature of things cannot possibly provide standards or criteria for assessing the truth or falsehood of new, contemporary theories, since if they could the dogma of evolution would be invalid. In the eyes of those who, despite its evident fatuity, still pin their faith in this dogma, a book like the present book, for instance, must by definition be a non-starter; for in assessing the truth or falsehood of the modern scientific world-view, of which the dogma of evolution is now the linchpin, it brings to bear standards and criteria of judgment that from the evolutionary view-point made their appearance in the human consciousness during phases of evolution long prior to that which saw the invention of this world-view as well as of the theory of evolution itself. This world-view and this theory of evolution must, therefore, for evolutionists represent a higher and more advanced state of human consciousness than the standards and criteria that I am invoking in this book; and the truth or falsehood of what represents a higher, more advanced state of human consciousness cannot possibly be assessed by standards and criteria which—since they made their appearance in what is thought to be an earlier phase of evolution—must on that account represent an inferior, less advanced state of human consciousness. Only if the theory of evolution is spurious could standards and criteria of judgment be valid quite apart from when or how they emerge on to the plane of human consciousness.

And we have the obligation to produce new theories of reality because by definition any past theories about its nature must be outmoded, since the level of human consciousness they represent has now been surpassed through the process of evolution. Hence they must be replaced with new theories which express the superior level of human consciousness that has now been attained. Thus we are treated to an endless succession of such theories, each as ephemeral as the one it displaces since they are all based on and determined by some metaphysical assumption, as rootless as it is arbitrary, which their authors have accepted unquestioningly because, one must suppose, they are not aware of it. A case in point is the theory of evolution.

For the theory of evolution, far from describing an eternal law governing the processes of the universe, actually represents no more, if no less, than a genuine though misguided attempt on the part of latter-day scientists to escape from an impossible dilemma imposed on them by their acceptance of a metaphysical conception of time—pure illusion as it is—as well as the kind of causality which inevitably accompanies it, bequeathed to them by their pioneering ancestors such as Galileo and Newton. Until this conception is abandoned, and replaced by an entirely different conception, scientists will not be able to avoid putting forward what are in essence metaphysical explanations of the nature of the physical world as fraught with self-contradictory, self-negatory and illusory propositions as the theory of evolution. In this connection it could be said that the theory of evolution itself provides far greater evidence for the *devolution* of human consciousness in the western world over the last few centuries than it does for its evolution.

Yet it is not that this theory, apart from its logical absurdity, is otherwise innocuous. If this were the case there would be little point in emphasizing that absurdity in so uncompromising a manner. That I have in fact done this is because its acceptance—and it has been so assiduously and effectively propagated that it is now accepted all but universally—cuts right across, and makes impossible the recognition of, a fundamental truth of Christian as of other spiritual anthropology: that man possesses the capacity to be totally renewed, or reborn, at any moment of his life, and this without there being any causal connection whatsoever between what he has been 'in the past' and what, after such rebirth, he now is.

In Christian terms, this capacity finds its correlative in the doctrine of what in English is rendered, somewhat unsatisfactorily, by the word 'repentance', but whose significance is more aptly expressed by the Greek *metánoia*, 'change of mind'. *Metánoia* means far more than regret for past errors combined with a pious hope that one may improve morally in the future—an attitude that might be compatible with the theory of evolution. In the full sense *metánoia* presupposes the irruption, or influx, into the psycho-physical organism of man, and hence into that of the cosmos as a whole, of a spiritual energy that transforms on the instant—'in a moment, in the twinkling of an eye', as St Paul describes it (1 Cor. 15:52)—one's whole being, so that one is, literally, reborn and becomes another and a new man, no longer the same person as that who committed past errors and now entirely liberated from them. The same principle is operative in the sacrament of baptism, at whatever age it occurs, as indeed in all sacramental activity. In fact it supplies the *raison d'être* for the whole idea of transformation which, as we saw, accounts for movement and change in visible things. Needless to say, the spiritual energy whose influx induces such transformation, whether in specific sacramental acts or in the internal states of individual beings, human and

75

other, is not subject to the so-called \law of entropy. That is why, for instance, the intercessions and activities of a saint may quite literally increase the energy-content of the universe.

In the present context the principle of transformation may be denoted in simple terms by saying that every effect that possesses temporal-spatial aspects has a non-temporal, non-spatial spiritual cause. What are perceived as movement and change in the physical world are the epiphenomena of changes in states of being. The temporal-spatial aspect of such changes are observable and may be accessible to mathematical measurement. The changes in states of being that produce these temporal-spatial effects, and are their causes, can be discerned only with the eyes of the spirit and certainly cannot be expressed in terms of mathematics. The theory of evolution, according to which changes that take place in the physical world, as well as in human and other consciousness, form part of a causative chain or series stretching far back into a temporal-spatial past and leading on into a temporal-spatial future, is totally incompatible with this principle of transformation that lies at the heart of all spiritual doctrine, and would, if true, mean that this principle is false and illusory. That is why advocates of the theory of evolution, as well as of the concept of time, or duration, that it presupposes, are of necessity, and whether they are aware of it or not, instruments of, and aid and abet the forces that attempt to subvert human understanding and recognition of a principle crucial to all genuine spiritual life—in fact, that attempt to corrupt human and other life at its roots.

It is for this reason that modern scientists who claim that they are replacing the machine model of the universe with something that is far more compatible with a religious or spiritual understanding of life, and yet at the same time rigidly adhere to the dogma of evolution, are more insidiously anti-spiritual than the straightforward materialists whom they like to think they are superseding; for they are forced to buckle and pervert this understanding in order to accommodate it to the dogma in question. A case in point is Teilhard de Chardin, a critique of whose theories in this respect is made in chapter five below—a critique which could apply equally well, *mutatis mutandis*, to the theories of his successors such as Rupert Sheldrake. But before embarking on this critique it should first be explained what conditions have to be fulfilled before any theory, scientific or other, can be said to constitute what may legitimately be called knowledge, and why not only theories of evolution but all other modern scientific theories as well so blatantly fail to fulfil them.

4 Knowledge and the Predicament of Modern Science

I REMARKED in the Introduction that one of the fallacies from which we have to liberate ourselves is the notion that contemporary scientific theories and the descriptions that go with them are neutral and value-free, and are not conditioned by *a priori* assumptions or presuppositions, specified or unspecified; and in the last two chapters I have attempted to show how the paradigm of thought that underlies the genesis and development of modern science does presuppose precisely such preliminary assumptions and that these determine its whole subsequent structure, as well consequently as the structure of each and every theory that derives from it. I have also attempted to show that these assumptions are purely metaphysical assumptions, and that their truth or falsehood is not accessible to any deductive or experimental demonstration.

What is implicit in all this is not anything very complicated. I may, for instance, see something which I can only describe as a ghost. My seeing of it is absolutely genuine so far as I am aware: the ghost for me is a basic fact. But whether I think it is an illusion or a trick of the imagination, or whether I regard it as an authentic manifestation of the supranatural world, will depend on all kinds of assumptions which in themselves have nothing to do with the actual seeing of it. Above all it will depend upon whether or not I believe in the existence of a supranatural world. If my philosophy includes an assumption that excludes belief in the supranatural, necessarily I will conclude that there is nothing authentic about what I have seen—I have simply been the victim of some kind of illusion.

This means that, paradox as it may sound, we cannot appeal directly to the facts to furnish us with any knowledge about them. Any knowledge of them that we may acquire—the mental concepts we form as to their nature and reality—will depend first of all upon the whole range of assumptions we bring to bear in our observation and assessment of them. We cannot, therefore, resolve the question of whether what we think we know about things—about facts—is true or false before we have resolved the philosophical question of whether our preliminary assumptions are true or false. There is no way of avoiding metaphysics except by refraining from drawing any conclusions about anything. There is no way, we repeat, in which it is possible to separate physics from metaphysics. There is not, and there cannot be, any such thing as purely disinterested scientific thought.

This is something that the modern scientist is only too prone to ignore—although in this respect, it must be admitted, he does not differ from the great majority of his contemporaries. He tends to be unaware of the metaphysical basis of his thought. He likes to pretend—and may genuinely believe—that the pursuits in which he is engaged are independent of metaphysics, or at least that metaphysics are unimportant so long as he gets positive results. He likes to think that he can possess, in certain fields, a body of exact knowledge, however small, about particular phenomena without presupposing any theory of their ultimate nature, or that he can know the part without knowing the nature of the whole. He likes to think he is a pragmatist.

Moreover, as the scientist's engagement in his pursuit demands that he adopts a certain method, he tends to fall into the idolatry of making a metaphysic out of his method—that is to say, to suppose that the universe is of such a sort that his method must be appropriate and successful. In this case he very probably is genuinely unaware that he does subscribe to any metaphysics, which is only another way of saying that he embraces his metaphysics uncritically because unconsciously. At the same time, as he himself has received his metaphysics through insinuation and not through instruction, so he will pass it on to others in this way, and thus the uncritical lack of consciousness is successfully bequeathed from generation to generation. The result is that with extremely rare exceptions scientists are not schooled in competent metaphysical thinking. Hence when they do venture into this sphere—or are challenged to enter into it—their performance tends to be pitifully inadequate, not to say totally inept.

A consequence of this is that when scientists do set out to try to explain how a knowledge of the physical universe is possible—to explain how, and starting from what, science reaches its determined conclusions—the initial data assumed are so confused and irrelevant that the theories of knowledge which emerge are such that one is hard pressed to know what 'to know' means.

Yet how, in fact, is a science of nature possible? How do you relate the mind that thinks to the reality that is? And if you make bridges between the two, how does this allow you to understand the mystery of the water that flows beneath them or of the terrain that they span? Faced with such questions, the modern scientist will tend to take refuge in the kind of evasiveness exemplified by Einstein's remark that 'the most incomprehensible thing is that the world is comprehensible'—a remark which, of course, leaves the question of how a science of nature is possible totally unanswered. And yet, as we said, there is no way of avoiding metaphysics except by refraining from drawing any conclusions about anything or—which is the same thing—except by ceasing to be a scientist.

It was this kind of predicament that so troubled René Descartes, as it must trouble anyone who thinks with any intelligence. For although as much as his compeers Descartes embraced the idea that the whole world of physics might be reducible to geometric qualities alone, none the less he still possessed, at certain moments at least, radical doubts about whether this could be done, or be done to any purpose. And the reason he possessed these doubts had nothing to do with the feasibility of the pragmatic problem of applying mathematical principles to the whole world of natural phenomena. It had to do with the metaphysical problem of whether the preliminary assumption of the idea—that mathematical 'truths' are capable of expressing the reality of things—was true or not. Could not what he calls a 'deceitful deity' have concealed the truth from him and have persuaded him to take for truth what is but consistency in error? For who can say that 'an evil genius no less canny and deceitful than powerful' does not compel us to take 'illusions and deceptions' for consistent and real exterior objects?

We are implicitly in the presence of the predicament that must confront everyone who is seriously and intelligently concerned with acquiring any form of knowledge. It may be expressed quite simply as follows: by virtue of what do I know that the preliminary assumptions of my thought are valid? This is the question that Descartes is posing, albeit provisionally, at the end of his first meditation: doubt about spiritual essences, then about physical existences, leads him finally not to see in the observing subject or in the visible world anything except illusions which one must expose as such. His deceitful god is the deceitfulness of the human mind when bereft of God; while his evil genius is now simply man himself who, he says, 'conspires with agreeable illusions in order to be more enduringly abused by them'. And if all is illusion, then the very substantiality of the self is put in doubt: it, too, may equally be a fiction: 'I could consider myself not to have any hands, any eyes, any flesh, any blood, not to have any sense, while falsely believing that I possess all these things.'

The modern physicist may claim that for him this predicament is no predicament because he must always check the truth, or at least the probability, of his hypotheses experimentally against empirical evidence. But upon examination this claim proves itself to be totally spurious. One has only to recall, for instance, the example of Newton who, as a result of the subservience of his thought to the preliminary assumption that the reality of the physical world is fundamentally mathematical, was forced to posit a conception of time and space that is as inaccessible to experimental as it is to rational demonstration. Similar examples of what are purely hypothetical notions about some aspect or aspects of physical reality are built into all scientific theories about the physical world. In fact, quite apart from the metaphysical assumptions that underlie and determine without exception every conclusion referring to the physical world that is called scientific, also inescapably built into every such conclusion is a purely hypothetical notion of some aspect of physical reality itself. It is literally impossible for a scientific statement about the nature of the physical world to be anything but hypothetical, whatever the degree of experimental checking to which it is submitted.

Moreover, what for the modern physicist constitutes empirical evidence is itself determined by what is purely a hypothetical assumption. For such evidence is said to be provided by sense-data. Yet this is to assume to start with that sense-experience is the sole, or at least the cardinal mode of conscious experience which is relevant to acquiring evidence as to whether a thing or a hypothesis is true or at least plausible. Why does the scientist assume this? In addition to sense-experience, and without taking into account our capacity for metaphysical experience, we possess at least two other major modes of conscious experience—those of the imagination and of the emotions. Why is the criterion in science for the acceptance of a theory confirmation by the senses, not by the imagination, not by the emotions? There is no possible way in which it can be demonstrated or verified that what we experience through our senses is more real and objective—or relates to a world that is more real and objective—than what we experience through our imagination or our emotions. There is no possible way in which we can show that what is accessible to experience through the senses constitutes more valuable evidence for the truth of our ideas than what is accessible to experience through the imagination or the emotions. And the evidence in each case is equally empirical.

That scientists do assume that sense-experience does constitute more valuable evidence for their hypotheses than other modes of conscious experience is the outcome of a purely personal prejudice. They could be just as empirical in trusting to the evidence of the imagination or the emotions if they chose to believe that confirmation by one of these two latter modes of conscious experience constitutes the most valid criterion for their acceptance of a theory. In other words, evidence for the validity of any idea, scientific or other, can be persuasive only to those already converted to the belief that it is evidence.

Yet there is more than this. For the very claim itself that modern science is empirical because its hypotheses must be checked experimentally against sense-data before they can be entertained turns out to have built into it another purely personal prejudice or assumption that determines what is regarded as valid sense-experience. As we have noted, the founding fathers of modern science were well aware that the senses themselves cannot discriminate between what is true in nature and what is false—the Copernican revolution itself was enough to illustrate this. The senses can mediate equally what is true and what is false. Hence, they concluded, sense-experience in itself is not to be trusted and the evidence it supplies does not and cannot either confirm or disprove any theory.

This being the case, some other criterion has to be found according to which we can discriminate between what is true and what is false —between what is real and what is illusory—in our sense-experience itself; and this criterion is identified with the principle of mathematics. Only what can be expressed in mathematical terms constitutes the real fact of nature; what cannot be expressed in such terms is irrelevant and does not constitute valid evidence. It is not realities in the physical world that we experience by means of the senses which constitute the empirical evidence against which the physicist checks his hypotheses. It is only the mathematical properties that the mind can discover in objects perceived by the senses that constitute such evidence. Hence what provides empirical evidence is not sense-experience or sense-data as such, but merely sense-experience or sense-data reduced to those qualities in natural objects that can be handled in the language of mathematics. Ultimately it is mathematics that decides what is regarded as empirical evidence, not the senses at all; and once again we are thrown back on to the metaphysical issue.

We can set this issue—and with it the whole epistemological issue as such—into sharp relief if we examine it more closely in the context of the character and competence of the cognitive faculty in us that is often thought to be decisive in the formulation of scientific knowledge, or what we call scientific knowledge. This faculty is the human reason; and we still tend to characterize the age that saw the rise and consolidation of the modern scientific world-view as the age of reason. We still tend to call one theory rational, and another not rational, or one concept reasonable and another not reasonable, as if the distinction in either case does not require any further explanation. We even assume that by the use of our reason alone we can obtain a true conception of things and that in this sense our reason is the arbiter of truth, with the necessary rider that what is true must be rational and what is rational must be true, while anything that is not rational is on that account false. Above all we still tend to call modern science a rational science. In view of this the need to establish the role and competence of the reason in the formulation of what we call knowledge is clearly a crucial one.

Here we may take our cue from Dr Johnson's definition of reason as the 'power by which man deduces one proposition from another, or proceeds from premisses to consequences'. This amounts to saying that the reason fulfills a kind of intermediary or mediatory role between one proposition and another, or between premiss and consequence. In order to operate, that is to say, the reason must have a starting-point or starting-points from which to operate: in order to get anywhere it has to start from somewhere.

Where it starts from is not self-generated, as though by a process of internal self-combustion. Where it starts from is, on the contrary, precisely an initial proposition or premiss that permits it to perform its task of deducing another proposition or a consequence from it. Without such a given initial proposition or premiss the reason simply cannot operate.

This means that however far back up a chain of reasoning from proposition to proposition, from premiss to consequence, we have to go, we will eventually encounter the original given proposition or premiss from which the whole process started. There must be ultimately an original proposition or premiss—what we have called a preliminary assumption—to every structure of rational thought. Such a preliminary assumption is what Plato calls the *arche anypothetos*,[1] which may be translated as 'first principle' or 'unconditional principle' or, quite simply, 'the Absolute'. In relation to the chain of reasoning of which it stands at the head, it is autocratic, axiomatic, uncompromising, and fundamental in the sense that it is inaccessible to proof, although it is itself, for the person who acknowledges it, whether consciously or unconsciously, the ultimate standard of all proof, of all demonstration and experiment.

Moreover, since such an initial assumption is not intrinsic to the reason, transcends proof, and is something that each human being has to accept and acknowledge—again whether consciously or unconsciously—as a condition of being able to think or reason at all, it follows that its acceptance and acknowledgement represents a personal act of faith. This means that at the apex of every thought-structure, theological, philosophical or scientific, stands an affirmation of personal faith, personal belief, in an assumption which constitutes the starting-point of the particular thought-structure in question. Such an affirmation of faith stands at the head of even the most positivist scientific explanation or demonstration, however elaborate it may be or however elementary and self-evident it may appear.

This permits us to make two further observations. The first is that the sense in which an explanation or a theory may legitimately be called rational is extremely limited, and that we commonly use the adjective in ways that amount to abuse, in that we apply it where it actually possesses no relevance and hence is meaningless. An explanation or a theory may be legitimately described as rational only in so far as it is deduced logically from a certain starting-point. It cannot be described as rational as though its rationality were intrinsic to it. Nor can its rationality constitute a criterion of its truth or falsehood, for this will depend upon the truth or falsehood of its initial underlying assumption, and on that the reason possesses no competence to pronounce. In itself the reason cannot be the arbiter of truth or falsehood.

The second observation concerns the nature of knowledge itself. I take

---

1. *Republic*, 510B; 511B.

it as axiomatic that knowledge pertains to the truth and that what is false cannot constitute knowledge, whatever else it may constitute. If we think something is true when, unknown to us, it is actually false, we will call it knowledge. But as soon as we realize that it is false we will cease calling it knowledge and call it a lie. A lie cannot constitute knowledge. This means that built into our very conception of what for us constitutes knowledge, and determining what we call knowledge and what we will not call knowledge, is the presupposition that knowledge must embody the truth.

But a thought-structure that constitutes a body of knowledge—the expression of truth in conceptual terms—is, as we have now seen, always deduced from a certain preliminary assumption. Thus whether it is true or false must inevitably depend, as we have also noted, on the truth or falsehood of the original assumption from which it derives. Clearly, unless this assumption is true, a conclusion or theory or system of thought that derives from it cannot be true either.

Assumptions of this kind, however, can be true only if they correspond to realities that are themselves true and not false, real and not illusory. This means that if we are to posit the possibility of knowledge that is true knowledge we have also to posit objective, ontological realities that are themselves real. We are quite unjustified in calling anything knowledge before we have identified the original assumption on which it is based and are convinced that it does in fact correspond to something that is itself real.

Such objective ontological realities cannot be constituted by objects of the physical world, the world we perceive through the senses. This is because the senses in themselves are of such a sort that they cannot discriminate between what is true in the physical world and what is false, between what is real and what is illusory. Consequently sense-experience in itself cannot be trusted for confirmation as to whether or not an initial assumption of thought corresponds to something that is real in the physical world. How we see things in the physical world, and the degree and type of reality we recognize in them, depend upon the state of our consciousness, upon the complement of preconceived ideas and values we bear with us when we come to look at them.

Moreover, as Plato among others has pointed out, there can be no direct knowledge of anything in the world of sense because, since this world is always changing, 'at the moment the person who seeks to know this thing approaches it, it becomes something else and different, so its nature and state can never be known; and it is clear that there is no knowledge which knows that of which the state can never be known.'[2] If the mind, therefore, turns for knowledge 'to the world of becoming and passing away, it forms opinions only, its vision is blunted, its opinions shift this way and that, and it seems to lack all intelligence.'[3]

This being the case, if we are to posit objective ontological realities, as we must if we are also to posit the possibility of acquiring any true knowledge, we must identify them with something other than the objects of the physical world of change and flux. We have to identify them with something akin to what Plato denotes as intelligible realities or to what St Augustine calls 'principial forms or the stable and unchangeable essences of things':[4] realities that are substantive in their own right, that are metaphysical and supra-rational, and that are independent of any human mind or minds that may posit their actuality.

For unless there are such realities there can be nothing to which the preliminary assumptions of our thought can correspond, and hence no way in which these assumptions can be objectively true, and so no possibility of our acquiring any genuine knowledge. To possess any genuine knowledge the starting-points of our thought must be grounded in the world of intelligible or spiritual realities. Otherwise they are merely assumptions that we have invented—figments of the mind—and have raised arbitrarily to being the starting-points of our thought; and assumptions of this kind raised arbitrarily to the status of starting-points of thought are, as Plato remarks, 'extremely shabby things'.[5] When this happens, he adds, intelligence goes by the board.[6]

Unless, therefore, we are to accept that by definition we are condemned to a state of ultimate ignorance in which the best we can do is to put forward hypotheses about whose objective truth or falsehood there can never be any certainty, we must affirm two possibilities. The first is that which we have just specified: that there is a world of intelligible or spiritual realities identical with or akin to that of which Plato and St Augustine—and many others—speak. And the second is the indispensable rider to this: that we possess the capacity to gain, through direct and conscious experience, a knowledge of these realities. Unless these two possibilities are themselves real, in the sense that they accord with reality

2. *Cratylus*, 440A.   3. *Republic*, 508D.

4. St Augustine, *De Diversis Quaestionibus*, P.L. 40, 29–30.

5. *Republic*, 506C.   6. Cf. *Republic*, 511CD.

itself, and are not merely hypothetical, and unless we realize the second of them—that is to say, do attain through direct, conscious experience a knowledge of intelligible realities—all the preliminary assumptions that we hold, consciously or unconsciously, and that determine what we think constitutes knowledge, will simply be assumptions of whose truth or falsehood we must remain incorrigibly ignorant; and, as Plato observes, if the ultimate ground or validity of the starting-points of our reasoning is something unknown, the conclusions we reach as the result of our reasoning cannot ever by any manner of means become or be called knowledge.[7]

Here we reach what is perhaps the crux of these considerations. We have already noted the limitations of the nature and function of the human reason, and have ascertained that it does not and cannot include the capacity to determine the truth or falsehood of the starting-points whose acceptance by it is a precondition of it being able to operate at all. Still less, therefore, does it include the capacity of actually knowing and experiencing—or knowing by experiencing—the realities of the intelligible or spiritual world, a knowledge of which is, as we have now seen, itself a prerequisite of our obtaining a genuine knowledge of anything else, whether this 'else' pertains to the mental order or to the physical order (in so far as it is legitimate to distinguish between the two). In effect, the reason in itself cannot know or experience anything—or, rather, it cannot know anything through direct experience of it, which means that in so far as it can be said to know anything it knows only by abstraction and derivation. What things are in themselves can never be known by the natural light of the human reason, and the reason itself cannot directly experience anything. As I said above, the reason is an intermediate and mediatory power.

This being the case, if the reason is to operate not merely in the name of purely subjective assumptions, but in the light of assumptions grounded in intelligible or spiritual realities that lie beyond its competence to know through direct experience, there must be in man an organ of conscious experience that transcends the reason and that is capable of knowing these realities in this direct manner. Plato himself certainly affirms that there is such an organ. If he did not, his thought would be self-contradictory: it would posit the possibility of a knowledge, one of whose essential qualities is certainty, while at the same time it denied that

7. Cf. *Republic*, 533c.

man possesses the capacity to apprehend the realities which alone can imbue knowledge with this quality.

Plato calls this higher organ of conscious experience the *nous*—the intellect; and the *nous* possesses a noetic power—a power of *noesis* (intellection)—through which it may intuit the realities of the intelligible world and hence grasp those principles in the light of which alone any true knowledge is possible. Indeed, for Plato, *noesis*—the direct apprehension of intelligible realities—is equated with *episteme*, science or knowledge,[8] and without it there could be no science or knowledge at all. It should also go without saying that Plato radically distinguishes the *nous*—intellect—from *dianoia*, reason.

This attribution to man of a power of intellection that transcends our power of reasoning and allows us to ascend in vision to the contemplation not only of the origin of our own being but also of the origin of all that is, and hence to know the inner reality and identity of all that is, is not peculiar to Plato. As might be expected, it is intrinsic to the thought of Plato's successors, the Neoplatonists. For Plotinus, for instance, the reason is able to reason to any purpose only on condition that it is in contact with and is illuminated by *nous*.[9] Unless the reason is intellect-directed in this way it cannot attain any knowledge, not even of the contingent realities of the world of sense. A true philosopher or scientist dianoetically translates insights he has attained when on the level of *noesis* or noetic awareness into the starting-points of rational discourse. Contemplation—the apprehension or vision of intelligible realities by means of the intellect—does not exclude reasoning. On the contrary, it is the intuitions of intelligible realities attained through contemplation that constitute the starting-points of any reasoning capable of producing conclusions that partake of knowledge. Unless these starting-points of our reasoning and rational discourse are grounded in intelligible realities, and thus correspond to things as they are in reality, they will merely be arbitrary subjective assumptions, the ultimate ground or validity of which is unknown; and in such a case, as we have already remarked, any conclusions we deduce from them cannot in any way either become or be called knowledge.

Exactly the same understanding of things is maintained by Christian

8. *Republic*, 511E; 533E–534A.

9. See on this question A. H. Armstrong, 'Tradition, Reason and Experience in the Thought of Plotinus', in his *Plotinian and Christian Studies* (London, 1979), chap. XVII.

theologians. Here I have to make a short parenthesis. Modern scientists who are also Christians, and who are thus faced with the task of somehow accommodating their commitment to the thought-processes determining the nature and practice of modern science to their integrity as Christians, often appear to be unaware of this whole tradition of Christian theology in which the ground-plan of what, from the Christian point of view, constitutes a valid epistemology is clearly established. Instead, in so far as they think in epistemological terms at all, they tend to justify as Christians their professional commitment in a manner that is as evasive as it is simplistic, as though the acknowledged masters of Christian doctrine had nothing in this respect worth saying.

Thus one is presented with a kind of syllogism which reads: 'Since God's creation is good, knowledge of God's creation is good. Modern science is knowledge of God's creation. Therefore modern science is good.' This syllogism itself may be buttressed by the Pauline statement that 'from the world's creation God's invisible nature—His eternal power and divinity—may be perceived by intellection in the things He has created',[10] in which the word translated here by 'intellection' is taken to mean the mind. Syllogism and Pauline statement may then be compounded and adduced as adequate sanction for the pursuit, by the scientist who is also a Christian, of modern science *on its own terms.*

This is totally to brush aside or to skate over the real epistemological issue. For the question that the modern scientist who is also a Christian has to face is not whether creation is good and therefore knowledge of creation is good. It is whether the terms on which, as a modern scientist, he thinks he may obtain a knowledge of creation do in fact permit him to obtain anything that may rightly be called knowledge, not simply according to Platonic criteria but also according to criteria maintained by the great masters of Christian doctrine. And as should be abundantly clear by now, this is a question that the scientist cannot answer simply by producing scriptural support for the pursuit of his discipline. And the same would apply, *mutatis mutandis,* to any modern scientist who claims to adhere to any one of the great religious traditions.

This conclusion will apply even if it is argued that knowledge of the physical world must be contingent because the physical world is itself contingent, and therefore there is no question of there being any absolute knowledge of it, or even of applying absolute criteria of evaluation and

10. Rom. 1:20.

interpretation to it. As we have already pointed out, the validity of what we call knowledge depends not on the nature of what is to be known—in this case the physical world—but on the validity of the unproven and unprovable assumptions we bring to bear in our attempts to know what is to be known. If these assumptions are themselves false—false in the sense that they assume that the reality of things is other than that which it is—then their application to what are regarded as the facts of the physical world cannot possibly produce conclusions which are not themselves false, however contingent these conclusions may be said to be.

That the physical world is itself contingent is something that is totally irrelevant in this connection. Statements about the nature of the physical world, and even the statement itself that the physical world is a contingent world, cannot be true even in a contingent sense, and thus constitute knowledge even in a contingent sense, unless the preliminary assumptions in the light of which they are made are also true.

But to return to the question of the recognition by Christian theologians both of the reality of an intelligible or spiritual world and of an organ of conscious metaphysical experience intrinsic to man through which it may be apprehended: like Plato and the Neoplatonists they affirm both such a world and such an organ through which it may be apprehended. These theologians are, of course, constrained by the facts of the Christian revelation itself to assign to things perceptible to the senses a significance that both Platonism and Neoplatonism might appear to deny them. But in this connection it should be remembered that in the process of initiation into the contemplation of absolute Beauty described in Plato's *Symposium* a role is attributed to physical beauty that corresponds exactly to the part visible realities can play, according to the Pauline phrase cited above, in leading one to a perception of invisible and divine realities; and the terms in which Plotinus describes the glory of the intelligible world manifest a spontaneous delight in the living beauty of the physical world that few so-called nature poets can rival.

Apart from this, however, what these Christian theologians say about the conditions under which it is possible to obtain a genuine knowledge, including knowledge of the physical world, corresponds exactly with the kind of understanding which characterizes Platonic and Neoplatonic epistemology. As, for instance, St Gregory of Sinai states, 'A right view of created things depends upon a truly spiritual knowledge of visible and invisible realities. Visible realities are objects perceived by the senses,

89

while invisible realities are noetic, intelligent, intelligible and divine.'
And he continues:

> A true philosopher is one who perceives in created things their
> spiritual Source and Essence, or who knows created things through
> knowing their spiritual Source and Essence . . . .. In other words, he
> interprets what is intelligible and invisible in terms of what is sensible
> and visible, and the visible sense-world in terms of the invisible and
> suprasensory world, conscious that what is visible is an image of what
> is invisible, and that what is invisible is the archetype of what is visible.
> He knows that things possessing form and pattern are brought into
> being by what is formless and without pattern, and that each manifests
> the other spiritually; and he clearly perceives each in the other and
> conveys this perception in his teaching.[11]

There is the same recognition of a cognitive organ in man—the *nous* or
the *intellectus*, again clearly distinguished from *dianoia* or *ratio*,
reason—through whose deployment he can come to know and experience, or know through experiencing, the intelligible or spiritual world.
The *intellectus* or intellect is that in man which most approximates to
angelic *intelligentia*, or to what in the Introduction I have called man's
higher or spiritual consciousness. It is the organ in man that is capable of
contemplating the *intellectibilia*, the 'invisible things which may not be
comprehended by the reason'.[12] St Maximos the Confessor calls it the
holy place and temple of God in man,[13] while for St Dionysios the
Areopagite it is the image of God in man, the divine abode wherein above
all God reposes.[14] According to St Simeon the New Theologian, the
God-receptive intellect 'is light and sees all things as light, and the light is
living and nourishes life in whomever beholds it'.[15] St Thomas Aquinas
describes the difference between the intellect and the reason by saying
that the intellect grasps an intelligible truth in a simple [that is, indivis-

---

11. St Gregory of Sinai, *One Hundred and Thirty-Seven Texts*, in *Philokalia*, vol.
4 (Athens, 1961), texts 25 and 127, pp. 35 and 57–58.

12. Cf. Richard of St Victor, *Benjamin Major*, Bk. I, chaps. 6 and 7.

13. St Maximos the Confessor, P.G. 90, 993 C.

14. St Dionysios the Areopagite, *The Celestial Hierarchy*, chap. 7.

15. St Simeon the New Theologian, *Second Catechesis*, 355–60.

ible, uncompounded] way, whereas to reason is to move towards an intelligible truth by going from one thing to another.[16]

Thus the truth that the intellect sees and experiences as self-evident pertains to the intelligible world—the world of divine archetypes, essences, ideas, exemplars or *logoi*, of which everything we see in the visible world is the manifestation and embodiment. No more for these theologians than for Plato and the Neoplatonists can we obtain any genuine knowledge of the visible, physical world without a prior knowledge of the realities of the intelligible world, for the simple reason that without knowledge of such realities we cannot possess any objectively valid (as opposed to arbitrary and purely subjective) starting-points for our thought from which a genuine knowledge may be deduced.

For these theologians, truly to know anything other than the realities of the intelligible world presupposes that we have already dianoetically translated the insights we have obtained when on the level of *noesis* or *intellectus* into the formal criteria which permit us to make that act of discrimination between the real and the unreal, truth and falsehood, that is the prerequisite of any rational discourse capable of leading to knowledge. As John Scottus Eriugena affirms, rational deduction is valid only if it proceeds from right contemplation—from, that is to say, intellectual vision of realities that transcend the reason.[17]

As for Plotinus, so for these Christian theologians it would be totally inept to suppose that the reason can reach conclusions which may legitimately be said to constitute knowledge unless it is in contact with and is illuminated by the intellect, and unless it is intellect-directed. Even St Thomas Aquinas, who distinguished between what he called the knowledge of faith (that is, of the intellect) and the knowledge of the reason in a way that subsequent writers could exploit in order to destroy the idea that the reason must be intellect-directed if it is to function to any

---

16. St Thomas Aquinas, *Sum. Theol.* 19, LXXIX, art. 8. It should, however, be emphasized that, as I made clear in an earlier book (see the chapter, 'From Theology to Philosophy in the Latin West', in *The Greek East and the Latin West* (Oxford, 1959), St Thomas's understanding of the nature and function of the intellect is very different from that of both the Platonists and the Greek Fathers in general. As I also make clear in that same chapter, St Thomas does in fact provide a complete rationale for the kind of epistemological approach subsequently adopted by the modern scientific movement, so that in so far as St Thomas's thought in this respect is Christian, this movement may be said to have its origins in Christian thought.

17. Cf. his *Periphyseon*, Bk. I, 511 B.

valid purpose, would himself never have conceded that the reason can formulate a valid knowledge of the physical world unless the principles directing its deductions are derived from knowledge of the intelligible world.

The spiritual intelligence—this higher organ of knowledge in us and the summit of the intellectual soul—is, then, naturally deiform and not simply an extension of our discursive reasoning power.[18] In its highest part it receives, when fully awakened, the direct impress of the eternal archetypes or ideas that constitute the inner life and reality of all created beings. These archetypes, or ideas, or *logoi*, are creative realities, causes of which each visible thing is an 'imitation' or manifestation. They are not concepts, or abstractions, or analogies, but are the spiritual energies issuing from the Divine according to which each thing receives its existence. Thus the spiritual intelligence knows all things through knowing the ideas or energies of which they are the expression. It is capable of a direct intuition of the inner and spiritual nature of everything that is, of which the visible form is but the outward mode, the apparent reality. Its way of knowing is through direct experience, and not by means of concepts or discursive reasoning.

Yet it has to be emphasized that this intelligence or consciousness cannot be operative and awakened in us, and we cannot share in its activity, unless we first of all free ourselves from alien attachments and persuasions, false and self-centred ideas and habits, and submit ourselves to what surpasses us, to the source of light and of the divine paradigms that only then can impress themselves on or infuse themselves into it. When our intelligence is cut off from this source, or has lost its roots in it, our experience and intuition of what always is, really and unchangeably, and of the inner reality and life of visible things, is frustrated and eclipsed, and there is no way in which we can know them rightly.

To trace the course of such an eclipse—the displacement of the spiritual consciousness by the ego-consciousness—which has in fact resulted in it being seriously believed that it is possible to acquire a valid (albeit if only contingent) knowledge of the physical world even when the efforts made to acquire it are not directed by principles derived from knowledge of the ontological realities of the intelligible or spiritual world,

18. See also St Maximos the Confessor, P.G. 90, 469c; John of Ruysbroeck, *The Adornment of Spiritual Marriage*, trs. C. A. Wynshenk Dom (London, 1951), Bk. 2, chap. LVII, pp. 125–27.

has been the endeavour of earlier chapters in this book, as it was also the endeavour of a previous book.[19] But what I hope this chapter has made clear is that—for reasons I have specified perhaps too many times —unless our attempts to acquire knowledge of the physical world are directed by such principles they will be doomed to failure from the outset; for they will then be directed by merely subjective and arbitrary assumptions the ultimate ground—and hence the truth or falsehood—of which are totally unknown.

Such assumptions can never in the nature of things be other than hypotheses. Conclusions deduced from hypotheses cannot be other than hypothetical; and what is hypothetical cannot be said to constitute know-ledge. Modern scientists may reject in theory, as they already do in practice, both Platonic and Christian epistemology: but if they do they must either accept that there can be no such thing as knowledge, even as relative and contingent knowledge; or they must make it clear, to them-selves and others, on what grounds they may claim that the ultimate assumptions governing their proceedings, mental and other, are not hypothetical.

Before concluding this chapter, there is one further comment to be made. This concerns the role of authority in determining what we accept as knowledge and the way we acquire it. It is sometimes said that there is a basic distinction between the type of mind that thinks that the only truth possible for us is that which can be acquired through free critical enquiry—or through an unbiased examination of the relevant facts—and the type of mind that thinks that no truth can be acquired in this way and that we are entirely dependent for any and all truth on divine revelation or its equivalent.

The first type of mind, it is said, does not know *a priori*, on the basis of some authoritative disclosure or document, what truth will be acquired as a consequence of a free critical consideration of the facts, whereas the second type of mind does know what truth is to be known prior to and independent of any examination of the facts. On this account it is often accused of applying exegetical violence—not to say of actually perverting the reason—in order to produce an interpretation of things that accords with the truth it has accepted on an *a priori* basis. The first type refuses to sacrifice its independence to any authority and is exemplified by the

19. See my *The Rape of Man and Nature*, op. cit.

modern scientist; the second does sacrifice its independence and is exemplified by the theologian. The first is said to be characterized by reason, the second by faith.

Sufficient has already been said in this chapter to make it clear that this distinction, and what it implies, represent a gross distortion, if it is not entirely spurious. Yet one point calls for further clarification. This concerns the degree to which the theologian is dependent on divine revelation in the formulation of what he regards as knowledge, and how in this respect his position differs from that of the scientist.

We have seen that before he begins his examination of the facts about which he wishes to acquire knowledge the scientist is already committed to certain *a priori* metaphysical beliefs, and that these determine not only the conclusions he reaches as a result of his enquiries but even what he regards as relevant in the facts themselves before he begins his investigation of them.

Such dependence on certain *a priori* metaphysical beliefs that constitute the starting-points of his exegesis is also presupposed in the case of the theologian. If I am a Christian, it may be revealed to me in scripture that Christ is both God and man, and this therefore is one of the facts that I have to take into account if I am in any way concerned with the formulation of Christian doctrine. But from revelation itself, and from scripture itself, I can learn neither how Christ is both God and man nor what significance this has in establishing the knowledge of the relationship between the divine and the human or the Creator and what is created which must form part of any coherent body of Christine doctrine. To assess these things I must resort to principles of evaluation and interpretation that I cannot derive from revelation or scripture itself.

Thus the theologian no less than the scientist has to accept starting-points for his thought which he has to regard as true in practice, even if he cannot establish their truth in theory, if he is to produce any coherent body of what for him constitutes knowledge; and he cannot derive these from the facts of revelation any more than the scientist can derive them from the facts of the world of sense.

This is to say that submission to authority where the construction of a coherent body of knowledge is concerned cannot be attributed to the theologian on the grounds that he acknowledges a specific revelation. Revelation supplies him with the facts with which he must reconcile his doctrine; but it cannot supply him with his doctrine itself, any more than the physical world can supply the scientist with the theories about it that he constructs.

If, therefore, there is a question where the theologian is concerned of submission to authority in constructing a body of knowledge, it lies in his acceptance of what he regards as authoritative principles for evaluating and interpreting the facts with which he is supplied by revelation. But in this respect his position is also no different from that of the scientist, who must also accept what he regards as authoritative principles for evaluating and interpreting the facts with which he is supplied by the physical world. The only difference between the two in this respect lies in the difference in the principles or preliminary assumptions that govern their thought.

To this extent therefore the question of the role of authority is a red herring in so far as the distinction between types of mind exemplified by the scientist and by the theologian is concerned. Both scientist and theologian equally accept authority, and both equally must believe in the validity of the principles which that authority imposes. In this respect consequently to say that the mind of the scientist is characterized by reason while that of the theologian is characterized by faith is also mistaken: both are equally characterized by faith[20] in the validity of the starting-points of their thought and both equally employ their reason in making deductions from these starting-points. Both aim to produce a coincidence between what they believe and what they think. From this point of view it may without any exaggeration be said not only that science is not one whit more rational than a religion, such as Christianity, that is rooted in revelation, but also that, in so far as faith characterizes religion, science is not one whit less a religion. That it is also, unlike Christianity, a pseudo-religion does not affect the truth of these statements.

If, then, the role of authority is significant in distinguishing the two types of mind in question evidence for this role must be based on other factors. In effect, it may be based on at least two other factors. The first relates to the status of the facts which the theologian and scientist respectively have to interrogate. For the theologian these facts are given to him in revelation. They are therefore God-given and cannot be gainsaid. It is consequently to what he takes to be the divine authority of

20. When Einstein was asked what proof there is that nature possesses unity, he replied, 'C'est un acte de foi'. See Paul Valéry, *L'Idée Fixe* (1934).

these facts that the theologian has to submit the conclusions of his reasoning, whether these conclusions pertain to purely theological issues or to their consequences where the understanding of the domain of nature and natural phenomena is concerned.

In this respect his situation is radically different from that of the scientist, who has no body of facts which he is obliged to recognize as authoritative and that are thus capable of operating as an objective check on the rightness or wrongness of his conclusions. For, as we have seen, the given facts of nature cannot operate as an objective check in this way because what constitutes a fact of nature for the scientist, or at least what he regards in natural phenomena as pertinent to the knowledge he is seeking to acquire, is already determined by the preliminary assumptions of his thought; and he recognizes nothing superior to these assumptions by means of which he is obliged to assess whether they are true or false. Hence the facts with which the scientist deals cannot be given the status that the theologian attributes to the facts with which he deals, the facts of divine revelation.

Thus if what the theologian believes with respect to the facts of revelation is true, then his situation will in practice and not merely in theory be radically different from that of the modern scientist, even if the latter claims that the way in which he intuits solutions to his problems corresponds to the way in which the theologian intuits the realities of the intelligible world. For if his belief is true, then the facts with which the theologian is presented are genuinely objective. They are not merely determined by the preliminary assumptions of his thought, as are what constitute facts for the scientist. This means that unlike the scientist the theologian does possess an independent and objective body of facts against which he can check, if not the truth, at least the credibility of his conclusions. If his conclusions contradict these facts, then he knows that either the starting-points of his thought are erroneous, or that the process of reasoning whereby he has deduced these conclusions is faulty. Of course, if the facts of revelation are not God-given, then he, too, will be in the same position as the scientist whose estimate of what he calls the facts of nature is based upon preliminary assumptions that are themselves at best purely hypothetical, at worst total illusions: he, too, like the scientist will simply be engaged in what is ultimately a wild goose chase.

The second factor which might be adduced as evidence for the differing roles that authority plays where the two types of mind are concerned relates to the status of the preliminary assumptions themselves in each case. We have seen that for the theologian such preliminary assumptions can be authentic only on condition that they are grounded in metaphysical realites that are themselves ontologically and substantively real; and that this presupposes, first, that there are such realities and, second, that we possess an organ of conscious metaphysical experience through which we can apprehend them. Yet this in itself begs at least one major question. For even granted that the preliminary assumptions of a particular theologian are authentic in this sense, how am I to know that this is the case?

An initial answer to this question is that I can check his conclusions against the given facts of revelation. But though these facts may constitute objective evidence in the way that by definition the facts of sense-perception cannot, yet they can serve to check a theological conclusion, to whatever sphere of reality it may apply, only to the extent that if this conclusion contradicts such evidence it must be wrong. This is to say that to be valid a theological conclusion must at least conform to the facts of revelation, and this does provide to a considerable degree a check on the authenticity of a theologian's initial assumptions.

Yet it is by no means foolproof, for—as the history of Christian thought adequately demonstrates—the facts of revelation are accessible to more than one explanation or interpretation without being contradicted, and hence differing initial assumptions can lead to differing conclusions without the integrity of the facts being violated. So are there any further criteria I can bring to bear in assessing the authenticity or otherwise of these assumptions?

I think that two such criteria may be adduced. The first is provided by what one might call the principle of concensus. If but two theologians are in question, and the theology of each, though different, is consistent with the facts of revelation, my choice of which one to trust can be little more than a purely personal decision between equal odds, though even here I have to bring to bear whatever degree of discrimination I possess. But when I am confronted with a multiplicity of theologians, none of whom violates the facts of revelation, the situation is different. For then I am likely to find that the theology of most of them converges in a way that cannot be accidental, and it is this concensus that can provide me with further assurance as to the authenticity of their initial assumptions.

To be sure, this is not foolproof either: responsibility for making a personal decision is never abrogated. Nor does the fact of such a concensus mean that theology can ever be a closed book or a kind of strait jacket: the

spirit of prophecy is inexhaustible, and new and more profound significances in things can always be disclosed, which means that initial
assumptions can always be grounded more deeply in the realities of the
spiritual world, or reflect new aspects of them. But these new and more
profound significances will not invalidate the principle of concensus: they
will extend, but not displace or contradict, the scope of the theology that
exemplifies it, and hence will provide further testimonial of the authenticity of the premisses on which it is based.

The second of the further criteria supporting the authenticity of these
premisses is one to which we have already referred, but whose conclu-
siveness we have not stressed sufficiently. Modern scientists set great
store on what they claim to be the experimental and empirical nature of
their discipline. Both words of course are connected directly with the
word 'experience', and both signify that which is derived from or based
upon experience, though in modern scientific usage the type of experience denoted is reduced to that which is based on and guided by
observation and experiment related solely to physical data or the facts of
the phenomenal world. We have already remarked on the spurious
nature of this claim on the part of modern scientists, so it is unnecessary
to speak of it again. But what is to be noted here is that this claim is made
solely with regard to the testing of hypotheses relating to the phenomenal world reached, in the way we have seen, as a result of making
deductions from certain preliminary assumptions or starting-points.

Yet these preliminary assumptions or starting-points which the scientist brings to bear in the choice and examination of his evidence, and
which determine the conclusions he reaches as a result of such choice and
examination, themselves remain purely abstract in the sense that they
are utterly impervious to all direct, personal experimental or empirical
verification. The belief, for instance, that the structure of reality is
mathematical, or can be expressed in the language of mathematics, which
constituted the cornerstone of the credo of the founders of modern
science, is a case in point: it is a purely abstract assumption, totally
inaccessible to any verification through such direct personal experience or
perception. It simply dangles, as we said, in a metaphysical void, the
ultimate proposition determining all subsequent propositions, and the
ultimate standard of all proof, demonstration or experiment, but itself
absolutely beyond all direct proof, demonstration and experiment. And
the same applies to all the preliminary assumptions built into the initial
paradigm of thought in accordance with which the modern scientist,

whether he is aware of it or not, postulates whatever he does postulate about the nature of reality, or of the physical world, or of consciousness, or of anything else to which he turns his attention.

In this respect the theologian—and here I use the term, theologian, not in an academic sense but to denote an acknowledged spiritual master of whatever religious tradition it is to which one is referring—is in a radically different position from that of the modern scientist with regard to his preliminary assumptions. For the theologian's claim is that his preliminary assumptions—those that constitute the principles of his thought—are not mere abstractions dangling in a metaphysical void. On the contrary, they correspond, as fully as conceptual images are able to correspond, to realities of which he has himself already attained direct personal experience. In this sense his preliminary assumptions are empirical and experimental in the way that those of the modern scientist never can be. And he can substantiate this claim with reference not simply to his own personal experience, but also to that of countless men and women, saints, visionaries, mystics, whose writings, art, lives and actions, even post-mortem actions, testify unambiguously to the same spiritual realities as those to which his own experience, and consequently his own metaphysical principles—his preliminary assumptions—also testify.

Assuredly, experience of these realities is attained, except in the case of very rare exceptions, only on condition that the theologian or his equivalent, or anyone else for that matter, has pursued step by step a path of spiritual discipline through which his consciousness and whole being have been delivered from their ego-bound state and have been restored to the plenitude of their original angelic or spiritual state. But this by no means affects or in any way invalidates the truth of his claim that what he says about the nature of reality is empirical and experimental in the fullest sense of the words, and is based entirely on his own direct personal experience and that of countless others. That the impresarios of the modern scientific movement have managed to persuade themselves and the world's public in general that the metaphysical doctrines of the great religious traditions are not accessible to empirical and experimental verification while their own peripheral theories are, when in fact precisely the reverse is the case, must surely represent one of the most successful frauds ever perpetrated in the realm of ideas. It is also a measure of our own intellectual degeneration.

The theologian, then, can adduce two objective criteria with regard to the authenticity of his initial assumptions which the scientist cannot invoke. For, first, the scientist possesses no objective body of facts against which his conclusions can be checked, since, as we have noted more than once, what he calls facts are already determined by a purely subjective personal decision. Second, he cannot claim that his preliminary assumptions are based on and derive from his own direct personal experience of the metaphysical or spiritual realities to which they purport to refer—to be able to do so would be to presuppose, as we have seen, that he has pursued a path of spiritual discipline to the point at which he is capable of such experience. Indeed, whatever his private religious beliefs, he does in practice accept as valid theories about the physical world based on assumptions derived from little more than the *ipse dixit* of some philosopher or fellow-scientist who neither claims divine inspiration, nor acknowledges a world of spiritual realities, or divine revelation, or the divine inspiration of spiritual masters who have interpreted and elucidated its meaning. Needless to say, these theories are entirely at odds with both the facts of revelation and their interpretation and elucidation by these spiritual masters.

The difference in situation is, then, fundamental and crucial. For, first, unlike those of the theologian, the starting-points of the modern scientist's thought—the preliminary assumptions upon which his whole subsequent theorizing is based and from which it derives—are utterly impervious to empirical or experimental verification; and this is to say that they are purely abstract, arbitrary and whimsical—a fact which inevitably introduces into all conclusions derived from them a similar character of abstraction, arbitrariness and whimsicality. And, second, these starting-points of the modern scientist's thought must be derived from a source other than the divine, for otherwise the conclusions derived from them would not contradict so radically the facts and realities disclosed both in divine revelation and in the lives, works and actions of countless saints, mystics and visionaries; and this in its turn means either that they have their origin in what Descartes calls the deceitful deity, in which case they are manifestly false and diabolic; or that they are grounded nowhere but in the pure subjectivity of the mind or minds that happen to invent them or to accept them—two possibilities that may in the end amount to much the same thing.

In any case such purely subjective and whimsical assumptions are, as we said, by definition hypothetical; and what is hypothetical cannot constitute knowledge. Only something that not only is true but also is known to be true can constitute knowledge. Or—to put this in a slightly different way—before we can legitimately be said to possess any knowledge at all not only does what we think we know have to be true but also we have to know that what we think we know is true. Short of this what we think we know may constitute opinion, speculation, conjecture, illusion; it cannot constitute knowledge. It is ironic, to say the least, that modern scientists, in order to describe their professions, have usurped the word, science, which basically denotes knowledge and knowing, while at the same time the very terms on which they pursue knowledge ineluctably preclude them from ever acquiring it.

5 Christian Vision and Modern Science: I. Teilhard de Chardin

AS ALREADY NOTED, a number of contemporary scientists now claim that modern science has cut loose from its Cartesian and Newtonian moorings and has abandoned the mechanistic paradigm of thought which I have outlined in chapter two above. They claim that their paradigm is much more fluid and elastic. Some of them would even maintain that there is, or may be, an underlying connectedness between certain of the latest scientific paradigms and the cosmological paradigms enshrined implicitly or explicitly in the sacred scriptures of the major religious or metaphysical traditions, and that an understanding of the first may help us to understand the second.

Such a notion would appear to beg many questions. Perhaps the chief of these is that it seems to be tantamount to saying that God, or the Supreme Consciousness, can learn from man and from the limited human intelligence. The sacred scriptures in which the cosmological paradigms of the religious and metaphysical traditions are enshrined are nothing if not God's revelation of Himself, and of the world that He activates, to those qualified or empowered to receive it. They are not matters of human conjecture and speculation. To suppose, then, that the human mind, unless inspired and illumined by God (or the Supreme Consciousness) can produce theories about reality in the light of which we can re-interpret sacred cosmologies might appear to be putting the cart before the horse.

In any event, although it may have become particularly acute in recent years, the conflict between religion and science, however much, for

102

reasons we noted in the last chapter, it may represent a misconception of things—for science itself is a religion in so far as it presupposes its own structure of personal belief—is not new in our culture. In its modern form it goes back at least to the Latin Averroists, who radically severed the connection between faith and reason, theology and philosophy, and asserted that philosphical thinking must be independent of faith and theology. It is in this secularization of thought that modern philosophy and modern science in general have their basis. Briefly, what this process of secularization assumes is that there are two orders or levels of knowledge. One is that which God may have of things, and which man can only receive through revelation—through the Scriptures, tradition, the Church fathers and conciliar decrees. The other is that of philosophy, a system of laws and rules which the individual human reason can discover within the purely natural order and which are adequate for the right conduct of life. This knowledge—human knowledge—has its starting point in, and so in a certain sense must always remain dependent on, the perception or observation of sensible objects. It is what later we have called scientific knowledge.

It was this split between two levels or orders of knowledge that St Thomas Aquinas sought to heal. Haunted perhaps by the traditional Platonic idea of the unity of knowledge, he thought that all views, however contradictory they might appear, could ultimately be shown to be compatible and in harmony with each other; and in his *Summa Theologica* he attempted to achieve this harmony. But once the notion that these two levels or orders, the one the object of faith and the other the object of reason, had been accepted, together with the notion that ultimately there need be no contradiction between them, it was not long before the traditional relationship between faith and reason was disrupted. Instead of the truths of faith and the principles according to which they had been interpreted in holy tradition providing the starting-points in accordance with which logical deductions might be made as to the nature and reality of the physical world, the human mind increasingly cut itself loose from its spiritual moorings.

Yet for reasons clarified in the last chapter, this by no means meant that the human mind was now free to pursue its enquiries into the sensible world unimpeded by the *a priori* acceptance of a body of assumptions inaccessible to experimental verification and operating where its deliberations were concerned as so many unquestioned dogmas; it simply meant that it substituted, however unconsciously, one body of such assumptions

103

for another. One of these assumptions was that it is quite possible to obtain a knowledge of physical phenomena apart from a prior understanding of the spiritual dimension and identity that constitute their reality.

This inevitably involved a falling apart, in human consciousness, of the spiritual and physical worlds, to such a degree that knowledge of the one was thought to be irrelevant to knowledge of the other. The final point of absurdity is reached when, science having been formally taken out of the framework of theology, theology itself is placed within the framework of science—within, that is to say, the framework of the mostly unspecified and purely secular concepts and assumptions that constitute the metaphysical basis of modern science.

This means that when there is any conflict between the conclusions of modern science and the affirmations of religion it is the former that provide the ultimate standard. In order to survive at all, religion must accommodate itself to the modern scientific perspective or simply go by the board. Scientific knowledge—or what is called scientific knowledge—is now regarded to all intents and purposes as the only knowledge there is.

Quite apart from the fact that, as we have seen, it is possible to call the theories of modern science knowledge only on condition that we pervert the norms of the human intelligence itself, this state of affairs has put those who still possess some allegiance to religious values in what is really an impossible situation. On the one hand their practical activities and, generally speaking, their thought conform to modes which have little to do with any religious understanding or purpose. On the other hand they confess to a belief in God and to the mysteries of His revelation. The result is that they are led to resolve—or to try to resolve—this schizophrenic state by tacitly separating religion from their living and their practical affairs.

This of course merely contributes to consolidating the schizophrenia. Moreover, it cannot but have a crippling effect on our creative life. We can live creatively only when our actions and our thoughts harmonize with our deepest beliefs. It is because of this that many in our time, acutely aware of the split between their religion and their life, and of the effects that this has, have sought to heal it by affirming, like St Thomas, the fundamental unity of religious vision and the modern scientific world-view. One of those haunted by the dream of such a reconciliation was the Jesuit, Pierre Teilhard de Chardin.

It is worth while examining in some detail the structure of this attempted reconciliation, because it not only exemplifies what was said in chapter four about the impossibility of any body of thought escaping from preliminary metaphysical assumptions, on the truth or otherwise of which will depend the validity of all that is subsequently deduced from them. It also exemplifies the pointlessness of trying to resolve the conflict between religion and modern science before answering the prior metaphysical or philosophical question as to the validity or otherwise of the differing preliminary assumptions in which the theologian and the modern scientist have chosen to place their faith.

Teilhard de Chardin saw it as his task to embrace the new view of man's history proposed by modern science and to seek to resolve the conflict between religion and science in terms of a new synthesis.[1] Not to do this, he felt, and to cling to what in this view are the now outmoded world image and human image of Christianity as if the theories of modern science had never been invented or at least as if they were of no significance for man's faith, would simply be to consolidate the split in consciousness that results from separating religion from life. Moreover, he thought that it is only by undertaking such a task that man—or Christian man, since it is as a Christian that Teilhard claims to speak —can contribute to fulfilling the Church's role on earth. This role, according to Teilhard, is to dignify, ennoble and transfigure the duties in one's station in life, to search for natural truth and to develop the scope of human action;[2] and if, he maintains, the Christian turns his back on the world and on the natural sphere of human endeavour, then the role which should be fulfilled by the Church—that of sanctifying each new age—is left to the children of the world, to agnostics or the irreligious. In fact, he adds, it is often such people who unconsciously or involuntarily collaborate in that building of the kingdom of God which is really the proper task of the Christian himself.[3]

If therefore the Christian is to carry out his task, or to help the Church to carry out her task, he must not turn his back on the world. On the contrary, he must attempt to see how he can reconcile and provide mutual nourishment for both the love of God and a healthy love of the world.[4] He must adapt the Christian system to the new perspectives

1. *The Phenomenon of Man* (London, 1966), p.283.
2. *Le Milieu Divin* (London, 1960), pp.20–21.
3. Ibid, p.40.
4. Ibid, p.23.

opened up by science.[5] This for Teilhard did not mean the building of a new Church on the ruins of the old, but the laying of new foundations to which the old Church could gradually be shifted.[6] Only when this was done would the two spheres of rational experience and of faith come into harmonious and fruitful conjunction once more,[7] and would that happy blend, thanks to which reason is harnessed to facts and religion to action, again be produced.[8]

What must first be grasped if one is to situate himself in the perspective of Teilhard's thought is that he accepts without question the modern scientific conception of time or, rather, of space-time, which, he claims, has been the great achievement of the last few centuries[9] and which, he maintains, is responsible for the intellectual crisis of the modern world.[10] Prior to the invention of this new conception of space-time men lived in a hierarchically ordered world whose underlying pattern was regarded as unchanging and in a sense timeless. But over the past four centuries this vision of the universe has been displaced by a view in which everything is seen as in movement and in which, he rightly points out, there is no place for the idea of the world as a virtually changeless hierarchic order. All life on earth is now seen as inextricably involved in a vast process of organic or biological flow in which every element, instead of constituting in itself a fixed point in a hierarchic scale, is thought to emerge from a previous element in an indivisible thread running back to infinity. All things that occur in time and space, all objects from the least molecule and the least of the protozoa to the most complex structures, are in nature and in position now regarded as a function of an organic space-time process, and neither the individual position itself of each object in this process can be changed, nor can its existence be suppressed without undoing the whole network of life. The whole process, that is to say, which reaches far back into the past and far forward into the future, forms an uninterrupted and organic chain in which not one link could have been displaced or exchanged.

Moreover, not only is man now capable of seeing in these terms; he is incapable of seeing anything, including himself, in any other terms. 'We are not only set adrift and carried away in the current of life by the

5. *The Future of Man* (Fontana Books, London, 1969), p.96.
6. Ibid, p.23.
7. Ibid, p.97.
8. *The Phenomenon of Man*, op. cit, p.211.
9. *The Future of Man*, op. cit, p.86.
10. *Le Milieu Divin*, op. cit, p.11.

material surface of our being,' Teilhard writes, 'but, like a subtle fluid, space-time first drowns our bodies and then penetrates to our soul; it fills it and impregnates it; it blends itself with the soul's potentialities to such an extent that soon the soul no longer knows how to distinguish space-time from its own thoughts.'[11] The sacred cosmological vision which had once inspired human life is shattered and deadened, and a new view of reality, no longer harmonizing with its perspectives, ushers mankind into a progressively degraded and brutalized world.

The revolution in human consciousness brought about by the invention of this conception of space-time, or duration, has, as we saw in chapter three above, its necessary counterpart in the theory of evolution; and indeed, for Teilhard, what makes the world in which we live specifically modern is precisely this theory of evolution.[12] That process itself which determines the position of every living thing in space, in duration, and in form, and gives the irreversible coherence to all that exists, is and can only be, he claims, a reality of evolutionary nature and dimension.[13] Evolution for Teilhard is therefore more than a theory, or a system, or a hypothesis. It is a general condition to which all theories, all systems, all hypotheses must bow and which they must satisfy henceforward if they are to be thinkable and true. Evolution is a dogma, a light that must be applied to all facts.[14] Scientists may still argue about the way things happen, about the mechanism of life's transformation and whether change or invention plays the bigger part in it, or about whether life has any direction and is going anywhere. But on the basic fact that organic evolution exists and applies equally to life as a whole and to any living creature in particular, all scientists are in agreement for the very good reason that they could not practise their science if they thought otherwise.[15] Alongside the new space-time concept, of which indeed it is a corollary, the theory of evolution is a categorical imperative to which all thought, scientific or religious, must adjust itself as a condition of its viability and truth. It is this presupposition that is fundamental to Teilhard's whole mental outlook. It is the cornerstone of his system.

What precisely does Teilhard mean by evolution? In the present context it is impossible to answer this question in detail, but the main principles of his evolutionary theory may be stated. The initial propo-

---

11. *The Phenomenon of Man*, op. cit, pp. 216–20.
12. Ibid, p. 229.   14. Ibid, p. 219.
13. Ibid, p. 140.   15. Ibid, p. 140, note 1.

sition is that in the space-time perspective the world in its present state is the outcome of movement. It is the result of a long process of transformation. Whatever aspect of the world we consider—whether it is the rocky layers that envelop the earth, the arrangements of the forms of life that inhabit it, the variety of civilizations and societies to which it has given birth, or the structure of the languages spoken upon it—the conclusion forced upon us is always the same: everything is the sum of the past and nothing is comprehensible except through its history. The world in its present state is the consequence of a 'becoming', a self-creation. Every form of life inevitably assumes a 'pre-life' for as far back as the eye can see.[16]

This applies not only to the world's material aspects. The soul, too, and even love, are involved in the same becoming-process and have grown out of the general movement of things.[17] In fact, nothing escapes this law. And nothing escapes either the law which is its corollary, that everything, in however an attenuated form of itself, has existed from the very first. The seeds of everything—and again this includes such 'non-material' realities as the soul or love—are contained in the world-substance from the beginning, and nothing that exists in any form we know could have come into existence had it not already existed in an obscure and primordial way in the past. Everything has a cosmic embryogenesis, although it may not receive the form in which we know it until a very much later time.[18] Thus, not only are there different thresholds which the world has passed across in its historical evolution—thresholds corresponding to a geogenesis, a biogenesis, and a psycho-genesis (or noogenesis, as Teilhard calls it); but also everything has existed, even if in a totally embryonic state, from the original birth of our planet.

To this initial proposition and its corollary, Teilhard adds two other propositions. The first is that this evolutionary process is not merely a haphazard affair, something that depends on the workings of chance and the indiscriminate play of external forces. It is not merely quantitative. There is an inner aspect to it, a qualitative aspect, a direction and a line of progress, so that though chance also has its part in it, at the same time the opportunities offered by chance are, as it were, selected in accordance

16. Ibid, p.57.
17. *The Future of Man,* op. cit, p.13; *The Phenomenon of Man,* op. cit, p.264.
18. *The Phenomenon of Man,* op. cit, p.71 and p.78.

with a certain positive orientation and axis. In Teilhard's view, it is impossible not to recognize, in accordance with the law already enunciated (that everything which we now perceive as existing has, even if only in an embryonic form, existed from the very beginning), that consciousness, too, must have existed from the very beginning. It is a property diffused throughout the universe, even if often in a state which prevents our recognition of its presence.

This means that the inner or interior aspect of things, or their consciousness—the two terms are synonymous for Teilhard—is not confined to man or the higher vertebrates; it exists everywhere in nature from all time. There is a double aspect to all things, in whatever region of space or time they may occur: co-extensive with their without, they possess also a within. And just as there are laws determining evolution from without—it is on these that a mechanistic science of matter may be built up—so there are qualitative laws that govern the growth and variation of the within of things; and science may ignore these laws only at the risk of reducing its conclusions to nonsense.[19]

It is this inner aspect of things that Teilhard seeks to include in his theories. In the earlier stages of the world, even in the nascent forms of matter, this inner aspect of things—their consciousness—must not be thought of as forming a continuous film, but as assuming the same granulation as matter itself. Looked at from within, as well as observed from without, the stuff of the universe is mysteriously held together by a global energy. Its two aspects, external and internal, correspond. The elements of consciousness and the elements of matter which they subtend, form a homogeneous whole. This is the condition of things in the first stages of the world's appearance. But with time, with the passage of duration, these elements of consciousness, present from the beginning, complicate and differentiate their nature.

From this point of view, consciousness reveals itself as a cosmic property of variable size subject to global transformation. The most decisive step in this transformation of consciousness on earth is marked by the first appearance of organized life, or the critical change-over from the molecule to the cell. It is in this change-over that the pre-consciousness inherent in pre-life becomes the consciousness of the first true living creature, and psychic life must be assumed to 'begin' in the world. It is a transformation of this kind which provides the key to the fundamental

19. Ibid, pp. 52–58.

law governing the development of consciousness: that the richer and better organized the structure is, the higher the degree of consciousness it possesses. Conscious articulation and material complexity are but two aspects or connected parts of one and the same phenomenon, and the more perfectly organized the material edifice the more perfect is the consciousness that informs it. [20]

We are now able to see what Teilhard means when he says that there is in life a continuous line of development, a direction, as distinct from a mere spreading out. The science which is concerned only with the exterior aspect of things has discerned two principles at work in the transformation of matter. The first is that during changes of a physico-chemical type no new energy is introduced in order to produce the change; and the second is that in every physico-chemical change, a fraction of the energy available in the world is 'entropized', that is to say, it is lost in the form of heat. This means that, considered from without, the world has a limit in time and will eventually burn itself out.

Once, however, the element of consciousness, or of mind, is included alongside the element of matter in the study of evolution, one then has to take into account not merely what happens to energy in the course of material transformation but also what happens to energy in the course of transformations in consciousness. One has to recognize, in fact, that though the energies of mind and matter appear to operate throughout both the inner and outer layers of the world in ways that are interdependent and complementary, yet it is quite impossible to establish a simple correspondence between the manner in which they operate in these two spheres. There is no hope of discovering a 'mechanical equivalent' for will or thought. One is therefore faced with the task of resolving the relationship between the inner and outer operations of energy in a way which does justice to both.

The solution that Teilhard proposes is as follows. He assumes first that all energy is psychic in nature, and then that in each particular element this psychic energy is divided into two distinct components: 'a *tangential energy* which links the element with all others of the same order (that is to say, of the same complexity and the same centricity) as itself in the universe; and a *radial energy* which draws it towards ever greater complexity and centricity—in other words forwards.'[21] That is to say, beneath and within the mechanical energy which he calls 'tangential'

20. Ibid, pp. 58–62.   21. Ibid, pp. 64–65.

—and it is to this energy that the laws of thermodynamics apply—there is another 'mental' or 'psychic' energy operating in the interior of things which he calls 'radial'; and not only is this energy not subject to the laws of thermodynamics but it is also constantly increasing.

The dissipation of energy and disintegration of matter remarked by the science which deals only with the externals of things is in this way more than compensated for by the gradual concentration of the world's physico-chemical elements in nuclei of increasing complexity, each succeeding stage of material concentration and differentiation being accompanied by a more advanced form of inner spontaneity and con-sciousness. Fundamentally, then, from the point of view of their interior, evolution is not simply an endless proliferation of things; it is nothing else than the continual growth of this 'psychic' or 'radial' energy. And this growth is marked outwardly by an increasing complexity and perfection of arrangement and inwardly by a continual expansion and deepening of consciousness, an increasing degree of cerebralization.

It is this relationship between the tangential and radial energies of the world, between the outer and inner of things—a relationship whose most complete expression accessible to science is the human brain—that gives us the essential clue to understanding in what sense evolution has a qualitative direction. It makes it possible for us to perceive that beneath the historically increasing intricacy of forms and organs there is an irreversible increase not only in the quantity, but also in the quality of brains. Evolution, through all its stages, is nothing but an immense ramification of psychic energy seeking through different forms to become more aware of itself, more articulate. It is nothing but a continuous rise in consciousness, which so far has attained its fullest development in the mind of man.[22]

The second of the two propositions which Teilhard adds to his initial proposition and its corollary is that this rise in consciousness which gives evolution its central direction has not yet come to an end. This propo-sition, Teilhard says, may seem to run counter to appearances. It may appear that the evolutionary process has come to a halt. This is suggested not only by the aspect of relative rigidity which nature now presents, as if it were an oceanwave caught in a snapshot or a torrent of lava stiffened by cooling. It is suggested also by the fact that the morphological change of living creatures seems to have slowed down precisely at the moment

22. Ibid, pp.62–66 and pp.147–52.

when thought appeared on earth. Moreover, to all appearance the ultimate perfection of the human element itself was achieved many thousands of years ago, so that the individual instrument of thought and action may be considered to have reached its highest state of evolution; and this is to add further weight to the suggestion that we have reached the limit of advance and that all things now have achieved their final form.[23]

Yet for Teilhard even if no progress is perceptible in either the physical or the mental faculties of individual man over the last twenty to thirty thousand years, this does not mean that the line of development is blocked. It only means that it must continue in a direction that surpasses the individual. Over and above the accession to reflection in the individual, there is another phenomenon of a reflective nature co-extensive with the whole of mankind. For Teilhard, the collective is always superior to the individual, the whole to the parts of which it is formed: this, too, is basic to his thought, and allows him to posit an idea of collective mankind, and a collective consciousness of mankind, that is superior to the individual human being and his individual consciousness, however highly developed this may be. Hence, though evolution may have come to a halt where the individual person and his consciousness are concerned, it can still progress in terms of mankind as a whole.

The individual does not exhaust the potentialities of his race, nor does he contain the ends of life in himself. There is something greater than the individual moving forward through mankind, something that is developing perhaps at the expense of the individual.[24] There is a particular form of mind, a particular form of consciousness, coming to birth in the womb of the earth today. The growth in industry, in communications, population, and other aspects of the modern world has meant that what had previously been scattered fragments of humanity are now being brought into close contact and are beginning to interpenetrate to the point of reacting economically and physically upon each other. The effect of this is that, given the fundamental relationship between biological compression and the heightening of consciousness, the level of reflection is rising irresistibly within us and around us. Under the influence of the forces compressing it within a closer vessel, the human substance is

23. *The Future of Man*, op. cit, pp.14–16.
24. *The Phenomenon of Man*, op. cit, p.178 and p.230.

beginning to 'planetize' itself, that is to say, to be interiorized and animated globally upon itself.[25]

Over and within our earth of factory chimneys and offices seething with work and business, out of the age of the machine and of huge collectivities and of science, a new and collective growth in consciousness is taking place. A kind of super-mankind is being born, a collective super-life. It is mankind as a whole, collective humanity, which is called upon to perform the definitive act whereby the total force of terrestrial evolution will be released and will flourish.[26] We must renounce the idea that each man contains in himself the ultimate value of his existence and realize that our purpose consists in serving like intelligent atoms the continuation of the evolutionary process in the universe.[27] 'The outcome of the world, the gates of the future, the entry into the super-human—these are not thrown open to a few of the privileged nor to one chosen people to the exclusion of all others. They will open only to an advance of *all together*, in a direction in which *all together* can join and find completion in a spiritual renovation of the earth.'[28] The advance is neither inevitable nor infallible; but its possibility exists. To mankind as a whole a way of progress is offered analogous to that which the individual cannot reject without falling into sin and damnation.[29]

In all that has been said so far about the evolutionary process, Teilhard claims that he is speaking simply as a scientist. He is looking at the facts—or at least (and this is a considerable reservation) at those facts which he regards as relevant; and he is not, he claims, going beyond what they can substantiate. In completing and crowning his evolutionary theory, however, he steps outside the scientific framework and crosses over into the sphere of spiritual interpretation. As he perceives, the theory as it stands so far is lacking in one vital respect. Although we may feel confident that we are given the opportunity of progressing still further along the road to greater consciousness, yet we are still ignorant of what awaits us at the end of the road, and of why we should endeavour to advance along it at all. There is no satisfactory outcome to the movement; and, Teilhard says, it is this uncertainty about a satisfactory outcome, and the feeling that there never can be any certainty about a

25. *The Future of Man*, op. cit, p. 308.
26. Ibid, p. 21.   27. Ibid, p. 17.
28. *The Phenomenon of Man*, op. cit, pp. 244–45.
29. *The Future of Man*, op. cit, p. 19.

satisfactory outcome, that lies at the root of the *malaise* of the modern world.[30]

What is lacking is a centre that can give meaning to and ultimately transfigure the whole process. And, what is more, to be able to give this meaning and effect this transfiguration, such a centre must transcend the limitations inherent in the process itself. If the final and resultant form of all our efforts towards greater consciousness is subject to reversal; if, so as to satisfy the law of entropy, it is one day to start disintegrating and to fall back indefinitely into pre-living and still lower forms; if, finally, all our acquisitions and achievements, in whatever sphere, and our own lives as well, are merely subject to the destructive action of time, so that the ultimate outcome we must expect is one of universal blankness or of cosmic death, then the whole impetus towards advancing any further is crippled and negated. So long as our acquisitions and achievements, and our own lives as well, are ineluctably tied up with the earth, they will perish with the earth.

The radical defect in all forms of progress as they are expressed in positivist credos is that, however far they may push the threat of annihilation into the future, they do not envisage any outcome which escapes this eventual annihilation. They propose nothing which definitely eliminates death. What is the use of positing even the most ideal form of golden age ahead of us if, whatever we do, it must one day disintegrate? For mankind to be liberated from its present discontent and sense of frustration, it must have before it a prospect, a focus, which is independent of the collapse of the forces of which evolution is woven. And it is in trying to clarify this prospect and focus that Teilhard leaves the realm of science for that of religious speculation.

The solution which Teilhard proposes as the consummation of the evolutionary process is really the crux of his effort to conjugate religion and science. What in effect he posits as this consummation—what transcends the process itself and confers on it its ultimate significance—is a reality that he calls Omega and that he identifies directly with the Christian Saviour. Omega or Christ is the outcome towards which everything tends, the term finally resolving mankind's effort to achieve ever higher psychisms. We have already seen how for Teilhard evolution is a continuing ascent towards and rise in consciousness, and how the crucial phase in this process was the awakening of thought on earth, or

30. *The Phenomenon of Man*, op. cit, p.229.

what Teilhard calls the *noogenesis*. This crucial phase does not represent merely a development affecting only the individual or even the species as a whole. It affects life itself in its organic totality, and consequently it marks a transformation affecting the state of the entire planet. 'When for the first time in a living creature instinct perceived itself in its own mirror, the whole world took a pace forward.'[31]

This step forward, explicit in man's power of self-reflection, is only definable as an increase in consciousness, and logically, since, as Teilhard has also argued, evolution is still continuing, it must culminate in the future in some sort of supreme consciousness. But that consciousness, if it is to be supreme, must possess in a supreme degree the three-fold quality which distinguishes every consciousness and particularly our own consciousness. This consists of centring *everything* partially upon itself; of being able to centre itself upon itself *constantly*; and of being brought *more by this very super-centration into association with all other* centres surrounding it.

What we are witnessing in the collective human world-view which is being propagated throughout the planet in our own times is an advance in the involution of being upon itself, an advance which is the first symptom of the birth of some single centre from the convergent beams of millions of elementary centres dispersed over the surface of the thinking world. The sphere of consciousness, or of what Teilhard calls the *noosphere*, is not only closed; it is also centred. The millions of centres of consciousness which make up the world are as so many radii all converging upon an invisible and supremely involuted point, a point which fuses them and consumes them integrally in itself. It is this point that Teilhard calls Omega.[32]

Moreover, Omega not only consummates and concentrates in itself the hoard of consciousness liberated little by little on earth by noogenesis. If its function were limited to this it still could not provide that inspiration without which our impulse to continue our advance must wither and die. The mere hoarding in itself of consciousness in an impersonal manner, if it involves the elimination of our own personal consciousness, is not something we can regard with any great enthusiasm. What man needs is the assurance that he can establish in and by himself an absolutely original and personal centre in which the universe reflects itself in a unique and inimitable way; and in addition that this

31. Ibid, p. 181.   32. Ibid, pp. 258–59.

centre is perfected, and not eliminated, in any higher aggregate of centres in which it may be concentrated.

Such a centre—a centre of consciousness—is man's very self and his personality; and for him to surrender that at the price of its extinction would in personal terms be a meaningless act. It follows that Omega, if it is to fulfil its function in a way that confers personal and unrepeatable value on our lives, must reclaim and reassemble in itself all *consciousness* as well as all *the conscious*. At the end of the operation, not only must each particular consciousness remain conscious of itself, but even each particular consciousness must become still more itself and so more clearly distinct from all other consciousnesses. In Omega, supreme union must coincide with supreme differentiation. In its ultimate principle, Omega must be a distinct centre radiating at the core of a system of centres. It must be not only the Hyper-Universal but also the Hyper-Personal, so that each of the centres which it gathers and guards within itself becomes through this concentration both universal and personal to the highest possible degree.[33] This it can only be on condition that it operates according to the power of love. Love alone is capable of uniting living beings in such a way as to complete and fulfil them, for it alone takes them and joins them by what is deepest in themselves. It alone is capable of 'personalizing' them by totalizing them.[34]

This is not all. We have seen that for Teilhard the function of Omega is to initiate and maintain within its radius the unanimity of the reflective centres of the world. It is to act as a universal centre of unification, and to do this through the power of love which it exercises. But there could be no positive relationship between Omega and the centres it is to fulfil if it were only capable of exercising this love in some vague and remote future. For love to be effective, it must be a present reality, not something far removed in time and space. Remoteness either in time or in space spells the death of love.

This is to say that Omega cannot be something that emerges from the evolutionary process in the extremely distant future and in total dependence on the reversible laws of energy which govern this process. For love to be possible there must be co-existence, and this means that to exercise its functions of reconciling and liberating the play of human attractions and repulsions Omega must be in a position to act with direct proximity, both spatial and temporal. An ideal centre, or a potential

33. Ibid, pp. 261–63. 34. Ibid, p. 265.

centre, could not act in this way. A present and real noosphere goes with a real and present centre. Omega therefore must be an entirely present centre. It is already in existence and operative at the very core of the thinking mass.

Moreover, as has been said, to satisfy the ultimate requirements of such action, Omega must be superior to the forces and laws governing the evolutionary process, and it must be independent of their collapse. If Omega emerged only in the course of evolution, even though at its summit, it would emerge with mechanical dependence on what precedes it. In so far as Omega is the synthesis in which the whole evolutionary movement culminates it will be discovered to us at the very end of the process, as the last in the series. But from this evolutionary point of view, Omega only reveals half of itself. Although it is the last of the series, it is also outside all series.

Thus, it is not enough to say that Omega emerges from the rise of consciousness; it must also be added that it has already emerged from this genesis. It not only already escapes from entropy, but does so more and more. Unless this were so it could neither operate as the mysterious centre of our centres *as a present reality*, nor be above the mechanistic laws of corruption and disintegration that science posits for evolution. It could neither subjugate consciousness to love, nor establish it ultimately in incorruptibility. In the final analysis Omega cannot be what it is unless it is simultaneously autonomous, actually present, irreversible and transcendent.[35]

From all that has been said of Omega one can see how Teilhard can recognize in it an essentially Christian phenomenon, and in fact identify it with the Christian Saviour and so achieve that reconciliation between the evolutionary and the Christian perspectives which he is so anxious to realize. Given the attributes with which Teilhard has invested Omega, the transposition from the one to the other is not difficult to make. In effect, he argues, God creates, fulfils and purifies the world by uniting it organically with himself. This He does by partially immersing Himself in things, by becoming 'element', and from this point of vantage at the heart of matter He assumes the control and leadership of what we now call evolution.

This partial immersion is accomplished in the Incarnation. Through His Incarnation, through becoming a man among men, Christ, the

35. Ibid, pp. 269–71 and p. 291.

universal principle of vitality, puts Himself into a position to purify, direct and superanimate the general ascent of consciousness into which He has inserted Himself. By a perennial act of communion and sublimation, He aggregates to Himself the total psychism of the earth. 'And when He has gathered everything together and transformed everything, He will close in upon Himself and His conquests, thereby rejoining, in a final gesture, the divine focus He has never left.' Then, in the words of St Paul, God shall be all in all, and the universe will fulfil itself in a synthesis of centres in perfect conformity with the laws of union.[36]

Thus, the Incarnation is a making new, a restoration, of all the universe's forces and powers; Christ is the instrument, the centre and the end of the whole of animate and material creation; through Him, everything is created, sanctified and vivified, His influence spreading and penetrating through the entire mass of Nature in movement.[37] Christ, in other words, is Omega; and the end of man's evolution is not disintegration and death, but a new breakthrough and rebirth, this time outside time and space, through the very excess of unification and co-reflexion of which Christ-Omega is the principle. The salvation of the species is not in any temporal-spatial consolidation or expansion but by way of spiritual escape through the excess of consciousness. The end is not *well-being* in any materialist or naturalist sense, but *more-being*; and the ultra-human perfection in which the evolutionary process consummates itself coincides in concrete terms with the crowning of the Incarnation awaited by all Christians.[38]

In this way the perspectives of science and Christianity are reconciled and it can be understood how the role of the Church in building the kingdom of God is linked ultimately with the evolutionary progress which the world is in any case following naturally.[39] So perfectly does Christian dogma fuse for Teilhard with his conception of Omega that, as he himself remarks, he would never have ventured to envisage the latter or formulate the hypothesis rationally if, in his consciousness as a believer, he had not found not only its speculative model but also its living reality.[40]

36. Ibid, pp. 293–94.
37. *The Future of Man*, op. cit, p. 319 and p. 98.
38. Ibid, pp. 316–17 and p. 280.
39. *Le Milieu Divin*, op. cit, p. 43.
40. *The Phenomenon of Man*, op. cit, p. 294.

This in brief outline is Teilhard's system; and it at once poses the question of determining whether its synthesis of science and religion has been achieved in terms which leave the religious point of view—in this case the Christian vision—intact or mutilated. Several aspects of this system do indeed immediately stand out as being diametrically opposed to Christianity. For instance, Teilhard's understanding of the relationship between the whole and the parts leads him, as we have seen, to attribute greater value to collectivities than to particulars. In fact, the whole of Teilhard's thought requires the concept of collective realities which are not reducible to their component elements.

This reversal of the Christian viewpoint attains its full development in the notion that for God mankind is a more important and a more valuable and complete category than the single person. This in itself would be enough to demonstrate the anti-Christian nature of Teilhard's thesis. But the main focus of any criticism must be the central concept of the system, the concept of Omega and its assimilation to the Christic function or, rather, the placing of the Incarnation within the framework provided by evolution seen as consummated by the Omega concept.

Here the first thing to observe is that to be true to his principle that evolution must form the starting-point and pre-condition of all our thinking, Teilhard is compelled to envisage Christ himself as involved in the evolutionary process, and so in that respect as subordinate to it. There is indeed a certain degree of ambiguity, not to say confusion, in Teilhard's thought at this crucial point. In effect, when discussing the Omega concept we saw that to fulfil its nature and function Omega has to be not only supremely attractive but also supremely present. This it can only be on condition that it does not simply emerge from the rise of consciousness at the end of the whole evolutionary process. To be supremely present and, it may be added, to be irreversible and so not subject to the laws of entropy, Omega must in some respect have *already emerged* from the evolutionary process.

Thus, Omega has two facets, or two halves. The one half is that which is disclosed to us at the end of the evolutionary process, and the other is that which has already emerged from this process. What is ambiguous, or confusing, is the question of whether this second half of Omega is ever engaged in the evolutionary process at all, or whether it remains permanently transcendent. At one point[41] Teilhard speaks of it as having

41. Ibid, p.271.

'already emerged', with the implication that it has previously been involved in it. But at another point[42] he remarks that, precisely to fulfil its motive, collective, and stabilizing function, Omega, the universal centre of unification, 'must be conceived as pre-existing and transcendent'. This would seem to imply that this second half of Omega is never engaged in the evolutionary process at all.

This ambiguity, or confusion, is not without its significance. If Omega were not outside the evolutionary process from the beginning, as a pre-existent and transcendent principle of the movement towards unity and convergence that characterizes this process from the beginning, from where did evolution derive its impulse to unification and convergence? During immense periods of evolution, Teilhard writes,[43] the radial energy in things, 'obscurely stirred up by the action of the *Prime Mover ahead*', was only able to express itself, in diffuse aggregates, in animal consciousness. Once, however, thinking entities emerged, 'the sublime physics of centres' came into play. When these entities became centres, and therefore persons, 'the elements could at last begin to react, directly as such, to the personalizing action of the centre of centres'. But again, unless Omega, the centre of centres, is outside the whole evolutionary process from the beginning, from where could the stimulus to become centres, and therefore persons, so that they could react directly to the personalizing action of the centre of centres, have come in the first place?

On the other hand, if Omega pre-exists and principially transcends the whole evolutionary process, as Teilhard's argument would seem to require, then this process must either have derived from it, or have its origin in another world-principle. If it derived from it, then Omega is its author, and so, apart from anything else, it is Omega and not evolution which must form the starting point and pre-condition of all our systems and theories, and whether evolution or anything else is true and thinkable must depend on what views we have about Omega. It is Omega, and not evolution, that is the Absolute; and it is in the light of this Absolute that anything we say about evolution must be considered. If, in order to escape this dilemma, it is now said that evolution does not derive from Omega, but has its origin in another world-principle, then there are two principles at work in the universe, and one has admitted a fundamental dualism in things, a dualism which, Teilhard states, is 'at once impossible and anti-scientific'.[44]

42. Ibid, pp. 309–10.   43. Ibid, p. 271.   44. Ibid, p. 64.

Teilhard might claim that these latter considerations go beyond the strictly scientific point of view to which he has limited himself, and that from this point of view all that is important is to know that Omega is already in existence and operative at the very core of the thinking mass. But if one is claiming to reconcile science and religion then the metaphysical implications of even the most rigorous scientific hypothesis must be scrutinized in order to ascertain whether in fact this reconciliation is possible. This is all the more important in Teilhard's case because, ambiguous and confusing as it is, his way of regarding the relationship between Omega and evolution is transferred directly to the relationship between Christ and evolution.

Thus Christ, like Omega, has two facets, or halves. In respect of one half of Himself He must be regarded as pre-existing and transcendent, though in this respect His relationship to evolution is left extremely vague. In respect of the other half of Himself He must be regarded, as we said, as involved in the evolutionary progress, and in fact as the final synthesis in which the movement culminates. This notion of Christ's insertion in the evolutionary process necessarily compels Teilhard to formulate the idea of an evolving Christ, of a Christ who is incomplete and whose final form is being elaborated in time together with that of all other things.

In fact it is precisely because Christ is still incomplete, still in the process of becoming, that the evolutionary flow itself is kept in motion. Through the Incarnation, Christ became the instrument, the centre, and the end of the whole of animate and material creation; He became its motive force. And since He was born, and ceased to grow, and died, everything has continued in motion because He has not yet attained the fulness of His form. He has not yet reached the peak of His growth. His Mystical Body is still unfulfilled.

It is in the continuation of this fulfilment that lies the ultimate driving force behind all creative activity. All human action and endeavour serve to complete the Body of Christ, so that Christ fulfils Himself gradually through the ages in the sum of this action and endeavour. Without this, without the evolution of collective thought, there can be no consummated Christ. He will remain for ever incomplete. Ultimately, and in a real sense, the whole evolutionary process is working towards the salvation of Christ. Ultimately, and in a real sense, only one man will be saved, and that is Christ, the head and living summary of humanity. It is the garment of His flesh and love that is being woven by the lives of the faithful on earth. It is

He who is the term and the consummation of even the natural evolution of living things.[45]

This conception of an evolving Christ, inescapable so long as the theory of evolution itself is regarded as the dogma of all dogmas and the standard of all truth, virtually stands Christian doctrine on its head. According to this doctrine, Christ is at once perfect God and perfect man, not in any potential sense, but as fully actualized and consummated realities. The Body of His Resurrection, His glorious or mystical Body, is already exempt from the conditions of duration to which the natural world—the world which is supposed to be in the course of evolution—is subject, and in no sense is awaiting completion at the end of time. It is through the sacraments and through sacramental activity that man may participate in the spiritualized reality of Christ's Body, and so complete himself. Were His Body still unspiritualized, still itself subject to the same conditions as those to which unsanctified man is subject, it would be incapable of exerting a transfiguring power on the natural world and on individual man; it would be incapable of releasing them from those conditions to which they are subject.

The sacraments, in other words, would have no ultimate transfiguring efficacy, whatever else they might have. To transcend, here and now, the limitations of death and corruption which characterize the natural world, man must be able to participate, here and now, in a reality already exempt from these limitations. This reality, in Christian terms, is the Mystical Body of Christ. If this Body were still itself waiting for deliverance till the end of time, were still itself waiting to be completed and saved, there could be no salvation for individual men and women till the end of time. The Resurrection and the ascension of Christ in His glorious Body would be not already accomplished, once and for all; they would be events which are to happen in the indefinite future. And the Eucharist would not bear witness to and be the consummated Body of Christ, and so capable of communicating its deifying energies to the faithful; it could only be at best a kind of anticipatory token or foreshadowing of a form that will not attain its fulness until the evolutionary process is at an end.

The notion that Christ's Mystical Body is not already a fully spiritualized reality would mean, if true, that the sacramental life of the Church is without any real foundation. It would also mean that man is

45. *The Future of Man*, op. cit, pp.319, 320, 323–24; *Le Milieu Divin*, op. cit, p.136.

not a substantial creature, created in the image of God, capable here and now of opposing and rising above the natural laws of the world through participation in the spiritualized reality of Christ's Body. It would mean that he is on the contrary a passive instrument of these laws, to which he must adapt and submit himself in the pious belief that in this way he is helping to save Christ.

Fundamentally, Teilhard sees Christ integrated into the cosmos, absorbed in the cosmic process. He sees Christ in biology and chemistry but not as He is in Himself in the divine Trinity. Christ the Logos, that pre-existing and transcendent 'other half' of Christ of which Teilhard speaks, remains a shadowy, even a token figure in his system. He is eclipsed by the notion of an evolutionary Christ. This notion of an evolving Christ—of a Christ who is still to be saved and whose Body is still to be completed—is a bastard notion subtly eliminating the divine transcendence and making God subservient to human interests and purposes. Admittedly, it is also a notion very flattering to human vanity. To assume that Christ—or God—has need of man's assistance in order to be saved vastly increases man's sense of his own importance, which is what he is always trying to do.

In fact, it is but a short step from here to reversing completely the Christian position and to saying that it is not so much man who is to be saved through Christ as Christ who is to be saved through man. This is perhaps really the secret thought which lies behind such a notion as that which Teilhard proposes, although it cannot be proclaimed so openly. Man can now think of himself as saving Christ in a vital and indispensable manner. Indeed, not only can man attribute to himself a divine purpose, but God actually has need of man. He ceases to be God, existing in and for Himself, however manifest He may also be in His creatures. The traditional Christian idea which implies, if not God's independence of man, at least man's dependence on God, does not of course contribute anything to man's sense of his own importance. But to turn it upside down, as Teilhard does, and to pretend that Christ, and so God, are dependent for fulfilment on the collective will of mankind, is radically to disfigure the original meaning of Christ and of the Christian sacramental vision.

It might be said that this charge fails to do justice to Teilhard's teaching. It might be said that unless such an idea as Christ's immanence in the evolutionary process is admitted, it is impossible to envisage the world as anything more than the 'dead' matter of mechanistic science.

Only if Christ Himself participates in the world He has created can this world be recognized as having an intrinsically sacred nature and as being capable of ultimate spiritualization or transfiguration. Christ must be concealed at the heart of everything; and, Teilhard's argument continues, if everything is still in the course of evolution, it follows that Christ, too, in so far as He is present in everything, must also be evolving. Were He already perfect—and so beyond the conditions of duration—the world would be deprived of any qualitative goal towards which it could progress in time. Evolution would lose its spiritual dynamic. Only by envisaging a Christ whose one half is not only immanent but also incomplete and evolving can the world be perceived as a spiritually animated mass in the process of transforming itself in time towards ever higher degrees of consciousness. Only in this way can it be realized how the world is gradually being formed into the Body of Christ and so prepared for that organic complex of God and world—the Pleroma —when, at the end of time, God will be all in all.

It is true that, as St Maximos puts it, Christ is ever wishing to perform the miracle of His Incarnation in all things. But this does not imply any incompletion in Christ. It implies incompletion in the present state of creation, which is by no means the same thing. It is here that Teilhard is led virtually to suppress another central aspect of Christian doctrine, that which concerns the fall of man. It is not accidental that Teilhard scarcely mentions this doctrine, and that in one of the few places where he does mention it, it is to speak of the 'exaggerated conception' that Christians have of it.[46]

The traditional idea of the fall does of course cut right across the notion of evolution, and the acceptance of the one must mean the rejection of the other. Christian doctrine not only posits a creation *ex nihilo*; it also claims that this original creation, which includes man, is, within the limits imposed by existence, a perfect creation. It is an organic complex of God, man, and world. Existence as we know it, and the conditions of time and space as we know them, issue from a disruption of this original creation. Life and consciousness have not emerged on earth as the result of any long process continuing through time. Life and consciousness are present *ab initio*, and it is their loss and obfuscation that projects man outside the state in which he is originally created, and plunges him into the fragmented and alienated world in which he now finds himself. Yet

46. *Le Milieu Divin*, op. cit, p.149.

this loss and obfuscation of life and consciousness are but relative. It is not so much that through the fall man is deprived of life and consciousness, as that they are now so darkened in him that he fails to see things as they truly are. The divine image is still present in man through the very fact of his existence; but it is present in, so to speak, a passive mode. Growth in the spiritual life consists in developing the divine image, inherent in man's very existence, in whatever time or place this may be, from the passive to the active mode. This development corresponds to the recovery of that life and consciousness eclipsed through the fall.

The essential point to grasp is that in the Christian perspective ultimate life and consciousness are innate in man (and, *mutatis mutandis*, in all created things) from the instant of his creation; and they remain innate in him (as in all created things) as a realizable potential of his being at whatever point in the course of history he comes into existence. In the Christian perspective, there can be no question at all of life and consciousness evolving with the supposed evolution of matter. Life and consciousness are integral qualities of the original creation; and they remain integral qualities of fallen creation, fully present in all phases of its existence.

The difference between the two states of creation, unfallen and fallen, depends upon the degree to which this life and consciousness are actualized in the one and in the other. But the possibility of their complete actualization is again fully present at every phase of the existence of the fallen world. This is why saints and prophets and sages may arise at any time in history: at whatever time in history a human individual may occur he possesses within himself the full potentialities of life and consciousness as well as the means to realize them in an active mode should he seek to do so. This is to say that the highest level of intelligence accessible to man and in many cases indeed realized by man is a constant and immutable and implicitly divine virtuality of his existence, not subject to change or in any way 'evolving' as the world 'progresses' in time.

Christ is not only Omega; He is also Alpha, 'the same yesterday, and today, and for ever';[47] and if He wishes to work the miracle of His Incarnation in all His creatures, this is not because He is in any need of completion—how could God ever be incomplete?—but because Incarnation is an essential mode of His Being and a manifestation of His original

47. Heb. 13:8.

glory. In Christ, creation is already transfigured. To the degree to which man remains impervious and blind to the transfigured reality of creation in the Body of Christ, he keeps the world in a state of fragmentation and alienation which is a reflection of his own fallen state.

It follows from this that if Christ is concealed at the heart of all things; if the whole of creation is impregnated with divine life, this is not because creation is Christ's Mystical Body in the process of being fulfilled, as Teilhard would have it. Quite apart from the grotesque notion which this involves of splitting Christ into two halves and of making one half subject to an evolutionary 'becoming', it also, in spite of Teilhard's protests to the contrary, involves a confusion of God and the world that either leaves God dominated by natural categories, or equates the world with God. In both cases the reality of the relationship between God and creation is misconceived.

Indeed, one may say that the almost exclusively Christocentric attitude adopted by Teilhard makes it impossible for him to envisage the full reality of this relationship. If creation is 'incorporated' into the glorious Body of Christ, this is through the Spirit and the divine energies which the Spirit manifests. The Christocentric attitude adopted by Teilhard, and inherited from western scholasticism, tends to diminish the role of the Spirit in creation, as it further tends to ignore the distinction between the divine Essence and the divine energies through which God penetrates and acts in all things. It is these energies, luminous radiations of the divine rooted in the heart of everything, that animate and transform the world—or would transform it did not man project on to it that opacity which is his as the consequence of the fall. It is these, too, that manifest the Divine Presence in the Eucharist, a Presence again sadly concealed by the fall. If the world is intrinsically sacramental, this is because the divine energies secretly circulate through the veins of everything, seeking to reveal to everything the miracle of the Transfiguration. To imagine that this Transfiguration and the perfection of the glorious Body are to be achieved in the unspecified future is to mutilate the Christian vision at its heart.

Teilhard's notion of an incomplete Christ, of a Christ who is to be saved, and his tacit suppression of the doctrine of the fall, are imposed on him by his need to accommodate the Christian vision to what in effect is his primary dogma, the theory of evolution. As we saw in chapter three, and as Teilhard himself recognizes, the theory of evolution itself derives from the revolution in our thinking about time. This change amounts to the replacement of an hierarchically ordered world-picture in which relationships are seen as occurring in a 'vertical' series, by a world-picture in which everything is seen as occurring in a 'horizontal' space-time dimension that stretches far back into the past and far forward into the future and forms an uninterrupted chain in which not one link can be altered.

Preoccupation with temporal succession has taken the place of pre-occupation with realities that have no past and future in the way that evolution demands. Not only might we again point out, as we did in chapter three, the manifest absurdity in basing what amounts to a whole philosophical theory on a space-time concept that itself is formed by a mind still on its own confession in the process of evolution, and still therefore immersed in the space-time world it seeks to interpret, and whose conclusions consequently cannot be more than the most tentative hypotheses. We also might ask whether this change in our thinking about time does not represent a further declension from the Christian vision, a further secularization of thought.

The more the Christian consciousness is developed, the more it ex-periences things as essentially reborn, or new-born, at every instant. This means that as one's consciousness grows the idea of temporal succession is increasingly replaced by that of divine instantaneousness. In the light of the mature consciousness, the past and future of things have little significance. Indeed, a condition of grasping the true nature of things involves rising above the notions of past and future. 'Let the dead bury their dead' and 'Take no thought for the morrow'[48] are the two injunctions which the Christian must seek to apply before he begins to see the world aright; and he begins to see it aright when he sees it 'in a Grain of Sand' and 'Eternity in an hour',[49] and when 'new every morning is the light'. Ultimately, should his spiritual growth permit it, he would see the whole process of creation from the initial *Fiat Lux* to the Parousia as a single timeless moment of divine self-manifestation.

In God, nothing is past, nothing is future; all is simultaneously created in the eternal now. The Word or Logos of God has an eternal birth, and the birth of all things made by Him is equally eternal: every particle of the universe is continually being recreated by the immediate activity of the divine energies. The process of creation is continually and every-

48. Matt. 8:22 and 6:34.
49. Cf. Blake, 'Auguries of Innocence' (Keynes edition, Oxford, 1966), p.431.

where being enacted 'in the beginning'. It is not something that has been set in motion in a remote place and time and that is thereafter operating according to its own evolutionary laws. It is a continual and ever-present 'opening of the centres of the birth of life' (Boehme's phrase)[50] in which each creature, however minute, comes into existence at the centre not only of its own space and time but of all space and time. As Blake puts it:

> And every Space smaller than a Globule of Man's blood opens
> Into Eternity of which this vegetable Earth is but a shadow.[51]

Indeed, if our perception—our physical sight even—was sufficiently purified and hallowed, we would be able to see and understand that no visible thing—nothing belonging to the world of phenomena—possesses existence or being in its own right, and that apart from its spiritual dimension and identity possesses no reality whatsoever, whether physical, material or substantial. It is this that foredooms to failure every attempt to attain a knowledge of the physical or material aspect of visible things—of phenomena—apart from the spiritual dimension and identity that constitute their reality, for what we investigate when we do this is something that is ultimately pure illusion.

The degree therefore to which we fail to perceive things in the light of the eternal present, but see them as subordinate to the categories of duration, indicates the degree to which our mind and experience fall below that of the mature Christian consciousness. It indicates the degree to which our mind and experience are estranged from the 'mind of Christ' and are dominated by what is 'but a shadow'. Preoccupation with temporal succession; the viewing of things as if they existed only, or chiefly, in a space-time continuum stretching far back into the past and far forward into the future, is not only a vast distraction making it impossible to see things as they truly are; it is also evidence of the density of the pall of ignorance in which we have shrouded our mind.

The radical distortions of Christian doctrine that Teilhard is forced to make in order to accommodate it to the theory of evolution, however, do no more than illustrate what we pointed out in chapter four, namely, the fundamental fallacy of the belief that, given its basic metaphysical assumptions, modern science is capable of producing any theory that represents or expresses a valid knowledge of reality. In fact, as Teilhard

50. See Boehme's *Three Principles of Creation*, chap. 4, 72.
51. Blake, *Milton*, Bk. I, 31.

himself admits, only to forget it in elaborating his system, all scientific theory is no more than hypothesis, and there can be no question of demonstrating that it corresponds to the real nature of things. To be scientific, a theory must fit the facts of observation. Yet when it comes to the point, what are the facts to be observed? It is a long time since scientists imagined it possible to observe phenomena in themselves, or even that there is a material world subsisting in itself which can be observed. As Teilhard says, 'our sensory experience turns out to be a floating condensation on a swarm of the undefinable'.[52]

Moreover, if on the one hand what was thought to be the observable world itself turns out to be a shifting field of unseen energies, on the other hand the notion that the scientist can observe objectively, as if he, with all his personal and subjective being, were not involved in the phenomena that he is observing, is equally spurious. This, too, Teilhard readily admits, though again he appears to forget it equally readily. 'There is no fact', he writes, 'which exists in pure isolation, but every experience, however objective it may seem, inevitably becomes enveloped in a complex of assumptions as soon as the scientist attempts to express it in a formula.'[53] Physicists and naturalists are now beginning to realize that 'even the most objective of their observations are steeped in the conventions they adopted at the outset and by forms or habits of thought developed in the course of their research; so that when they reach the end of their analyses they cannot tell with any certainty whether the structure they have reached is the essence of the matter they are studying, or the reflection of their own thought . . .. Man willy-nilly finds his own image stamped on all he looks at'.[54] In other words, the facts of observation in physics or biology are not objective phenomena, but phenomena submitted to human interrogation where man encounters only the reflection of his own thought and its formulas.

In the light of this the fundamental fallacy implicit in Teilhard's as in any other attempt to reconcile modern science with religion is clearly evident. The theory about man and his destiny which he propounds and to which he so ruthlessly adapts Christianity is not, as he claims it is, purely and simply scientific, purely a matter of scientific reflection or verified by objective observation;[55] it is but the conjecture of a mind committed to looking at things in a certain way because of its implicit

---

52. *The Phenomenon of Man*, op. cit, p.41.
53. Ibid, p.30.   54. Ibid, p.32.   55. Ibid, p.29.

categories of thought and response and the personal character of the thinker himself. It is the presuppositions which the thinker bears with him as a person, often at a level of which he is unaware or which, when he is aware of it, he is unable to specify, that provide the framework within which and according to which he interprets what he observes. It is well said that the eye sees in things only what it looks for and it looks only for what it already has in mind.

Ultimately the conflict between modern science and religion is not between theories and ideas that are objectively verifiable and those that transcend such verification, or between reason and faith. It is between different kinds of faith, between what authority one accepts as providing an adequate ground for thought and action in the first place, and the strength with which one believes in it. This is only another way of saying that as one is, so one will see the world. A person who accepts as the ground of his reasoning a proposition purely secular in character will produce a picture of the universe which is itself as purely secular as he can make it. A person who denies the divine image in himself will effectively estrange himself from it, and will see the world as a spiritless desert. It is the meaning one confers on things that finally determines their significance for one and even their appearance, since in the end what the world looks like to us depends on the image we impose upon it.

As we made clear in the last chapter, this does not in the least mean that all theories and ideas are equally hypothetical, and that no one way of seeing things is more true than other ways. But it should help to make one aware of the limitations of what are put forward as scientific theories, as well as of how totally inadequate these are to provide standards according to which the truth of a religious doctrine can be measured or modified. It should help also to re-emphasize that if there is any theory or idea that is more than hypothetical then it can only derive from a source that is itself more than hypothetical; and that it is this theory or idea that must provide the final standard for assessing the value of all other theories and ideas, whatever may be the scientific standing and authority attributed to them.

6 Christian Vision and Modern Science: II. Oskar Milosz

WE HAVE PRESENTED the ascendancy of the paradigm of thought that determines what has become the dominant world-view of modern times as signifying the death of sacred cosmology; and we have seen that the attempt to revive such a cosmology by trying to reconcile a spiritual vision of the universe with the metaphysical presuppositions embedded in that paradigm can only result in mutilating such a vision at its heart: there can in the nature of things be no reconciliation between the Christian or any other sacred cosmology and the modern scientific world-view for the simple reason that the metaphysical presuppositions on which this world-view is based are themselves totally non-spiritual. This is tantamount to saying that a revival of a spiritual understanding of the physical world can come about only on condition that these presuppositions are rejected, and are replaced by those that underlie the cosmologies of the great sacred religions.

Yet in spite of the ascendancy, now virtually world-wide, of the materialistic and positivist scientism established by scientists like Copernicus, Galileo and Newton in the sixteenth and seventeenth centuries, there have always been those in Europe who have been aware that such scientism represents a radical warping of the human intelligence and hence must issue in a correspondingly distorted view of the natural world. Concomitantly they have been aware that there can be no true science of phenomena—of visible nature—that is not based on and rooted in a science of the spiritual realities of which visible phenomena are the spatio-temporal manifestations or 'signatures'; and that consequently a

131

knowledge of these metaphysical realities is a prerequisite of a knowledge of their physical analogues in the natural world. This 'other mind of Europe', as it has been called,[1] has been exemplified in alchemical and experimental works by such figures as the sixteenth-century Swiss *magus*, Paracelsus, Robert Fludd and Goethe, and it has been given philosophical and imaginative expression by the seventeenth-century Cambridge Platonists, by Thomas Traherne, and by visionaries such as Boehme, Swedenborg, Claude de Saint Martin, Bishop Berkeley and William Blake. A more recent representative of this mystical, imaginative and profoundly experiential tradition is the poet and visionary, Oskar Milosz (1877–1939).[2]

What is Milosz's vision in so far as it relates to the thesis of this book, and why is it so important? He himself described his mission as the renewal of Christian metaphysics and as the annunciation of a future Christianity. At the same time he claimed that his doctrine did not in the least degree differ from traditional Christian doctrine, and clearly the last thing he wished was to establish a new form of Christianity or a new religion of any kind. Rather, what he attempted to do was to diagnose why the spiritual universe of western man—essentially and inevitably, he thought, a Christian universe—had been shattered and man himself ejected into a kind of infernal void; and to reaffirm the metaphysical principles whose rejection had produced this state of affairs and whose reaffirmation is a precondition of any spiritual or artistic renewal. The dedication of one of his major works, *Ars Magna*, to 'my spouse Renaissance' testifies to his deep hope in the possibility of such a renewal—an era of reborn humanity to which his own works were to be an immediate and crucial contribution. Indeed, he saw no point in any art, science or philosophy that did not contribute directly and consciously to such a rebirth—that was not, in other words, devoted to the promotion of religion and spiritual knowledge. Any art not so devoted, he confessed, whether poetry, music or painting, 'makes me shudder with unspeakable horror'.

Milosz's diagnosis of the abysmal state of present-day humanity has

1. By J. P. S. Uberoi. See his *The Other Mind of Europe* (Delhi, 1984).

2. For a comprehensive selection of Milosz's writings, translated into English, see *The Noble Traveller. The Life and Writings of O. V. de L. Milosz*, ed. and selected by Christopher Bamford, Introduction by Czeslaw Milosz (Lindisfarne Press, Massachusetts, 1985). The summary of Milosz's doctrine presented in this chapter is based on this work.

its start in a proposition which he accepts as axiomatic. This is that our spiritual potentiality—our true being—cannot be actualized unless the way in which we represent to ourselves the physical universe and man's place in it accords with things as they are in reality. In other words—to put the same thing in more specifically Christian terms—there must be a correspondence between the way in which God actually creates and sustains the world and the way in which we ourselves conceive it if we are to realize the relationship with and participation in the divine that is also the reality of our own innermost being. There must be an awareness that human destiny and salvation, and the destiny and salvation of the world, are inextricably interconnected. Unless there is such an awareness we become victims of an inner dislocation and blindness which imprison us in a false vision of our life and of the life of things about us and produce a chronic perversion in every aspect of our existence and activity, spiritual, psychological, physical, artistic and social.

Such a dislocation and blindness have in fact been brought about, according to Milosz, by our acceptance of the world-view of modern science. Man's deepest need—that which corresponds to the innermost reality of his being and on whose realization depends his release from a state of anguish, torment and mental and physical disease—is to live and love eternally. Yet modern science has presented him with a concept of the universe in which this is an impossibility, for the simple reason that, according to this concept, everything inevitably has a beginning and an end. 'Ever since the first victory of materialism over revealed truth', Milosz writes, 'our concept of space and consequently, of the universe and of life, which space seems to contain, has been absolutely incompatible with the healthy logic surviving intact in the depth of our latent memory. Man, created free, has materialized his secret being and, together with it, Nature in the universal sense of the word. His folly has prompted him to *situate* the containing space to which he has ascribed a real existence; this space, in his sacrilegious thought, became stretched to infinity and became identified with the spiritual absolute. Now, this precisely is Hell . . .'—in other words, imprisonment without release in a state of anguish, torment and mental and physical disease.

Put in its simplest terms, what Milosz calls our criminal pride has led us to propose a totally unreal connection between the idea of space and that of the infinite. Hence, in our modern view of things, space—identified with the container of all life—appears to us as an immense curtain of darkness hanging in an eternity of time. In thus identifying the absolute with space and eternity with time, both determinable by endless multi-plication and division, and in crowning ourselves king of the infinite universe-space situated by itself in endless extension—a universe of matter situated in itself—we have effectively deprived ourselves of any place in which the basic needs of our own being can be expressed, let alone fulfilled. For what we have done, when stripped to its bare reality, is to proclaim ourselves sovereign for a day of a lump of matter sentenced to slow decay in the darkness of a death without beginning or end. There is literally nowhere where we can live and love eternally: we are not situated anywhere, have nowhere to lay our head, we are lost, astray in this false space which is but our own illusion, our own animation of what is not actually there, eternally displaced, rootless, dispossessed.

Hence our endless psychoses, our atrocious metaphysical terror, our frenzy and torment, absolutely inescapable so long as we persist in clinging to this false and sacrilegious concept of the world and our own existence in it. In other words, the space-time concept of modern science, accompanied as it necessarily is by what Milosz calls the great illusion of evolution—the concept, in short, regarded by virtually all modern scientists as a completely unchallengeable dogma—is in reality a torture-chamber in which we endlessly punish ourselves for our self-apostasy and self-blinding.

The first stage therefore in any recovery of true identity on our part is to free ourselves from this tyrannical illusion in which we have become entangled and which lacks all reality except that conferred on it by our own deluded mind. We have, literally, to change our mind. And the first sign that we are beginning to do this is that we start to ask ourselves seriously, not 'What am I?', but 'Where am I?' Modern science can answer only that we exist in space, or in space-time. But this is to beg the question, because in that case where is space itself situated? For unless the question, 'Where is space?', is answered we cannot escape from the infinity of darkness in which the world-view of modern science places us.

Modern science, of course, cannot answer this question for us and must declare its impotence when faced with it. But neither can any metaphysical doctrine or religious teaching which suggests that it matters little how we conceive the physical universe either because all mental constructs are basically delusion or because the spiritual world is opposed to the physical world and exists on an entirely different plane, so that whatever the idea we may possess of the physical world it does not inhibit our capacity to live a full spiritual life. For Milosz, both these attitudes contradict his basic axiom, indicated at the start of this *résumé* of his thought, that unless man's concept of the physical universe does accord with reality, his spiritual life will be crippled at its roots, with devastating consequences for every other aspect of his life. The modern world would seem amply to verify this contention.

Hence it is not simply a matter of demonstrating the unreality of the modern scientific world-view; it is a matter also of affirming a concept of the physical universe and of our place in it, down to the most seemingly insignificant aspects of our physical life, that is in accord with reality and corresponds consequently with our deepest and most ineluctable being. Initially, this means a reshaping of our concept of space and time, or, rather, of space, time and matter, since these are the three basic elements of the modern scientific concept and Milosz's avowed intention was to metamorphose this concept. Yet so ingrained are the centuries-old habits of our mind that it is by no means easy for us to grasp the metamorphosis which he proposes: as he himself writes, it is easier to preach the truth to trees and rocks than to make people grasp it.

Yet we have already advanced some way towards understanding what it is by perceiving what it is not. As we have seen, for Milosz the basic perversion of human thought is the absurd and criminal identification of the infinite with space—in other words, the identification of space with the absolute. This idea of space—the idea of a space extended to infinity, with all its darkness, cold, and insensibility—and its corresponding idea of an eternity of succession divided into past, present and future, are indeed, Milosz states, Satan himself in all the immense black majesty of his terrors. As for Berkeley, so for Milosz such an idea of absolute space is a phantom of the mechanical philosophers, and like Blake he saw the 'fathomless void' implicit in such an idea as the 'soul-shuddering vacuum' into which the human mind plunges when its intellectual sight is blinded and it loses contact with the real world of vision. It is of course also this idea of space that has given rise to all those cosmogonies —equally false—that presume that the universe is the outcome of some kind of organization of chaos within a pre-existing void, as though there were a prior and pre-existing receptacle or container into which the waters of space-time could be poured.

The materialization of thought which such a concept of space-time presupposes—this multiplication and division to infinity in a vain attempt to fill a black eternity of terror by locating an infinitude of cosmic points in a movement cut automatically into the three slices of past, present and future—amounts to a lapse into the darkness of the infernal world in which we have the illusion of ruling over a universe situated in its own matter. But if this concept of a monstrous material deity extending to infinity is not only wrong but also positively evil, in that it perverts and deforms the actual truth and reality of things, with what concept does one supplant it?

As a Christian, central to Milosz's thought is the traditional Christian idea of the Incarnation, an idea which involves the recognition, in his own words, 'that the matter which clothes us and surrounds us is absolutely identical with that in which all-powerful Love humbled Himself during the years of the Incarnation,' and which He continues to hallow, he might have added, at every celebration of the Eucharist. He could not therefore respond to the 'universe of death' promoted by such as Locke and Newton in quite the same way as, for instance, Berkeley and Blake, however much he would have agreed with them in condemning it. He had to wage his battle as it were on two fronts, first and foremost against the materialists, but also against the exponents of what one can describe as immaterialist philosophy. This is the kind of philosophy which affirms that the material world has no reality apart from the mind that perceives it—has no reality independent of mental perception—and that consequently the existence of material things or sensible objects is dependent upon their being perceived: their *esse* is *percipi*. Blake, following Berkeley in this respect, is expressing such a philosophy when he states in a typically aphoristic manner: 'Mental Things are alone Real; what is call'd Corporeal, Nobody Knows of its Dwelling Place: it is in Fallacy, & its Existence an Imposture.'[3]

Moreover, to reduce the physical universe to a category that has no existence distinct from being perceived by the human mind comes dangerously close to investing man with a sovereignty even more flattering to his ego than that with which modern science invests him. For once I accept the idea that what is called the material world—the world immediately accessible to our senses—exists only in the mind and that mental things alone are real while all the rest is illusion, it is but a short step to my assuming that my own purely subjective mental state is the supreme arbiter of things and determines their true nature, and that how I see the universe is consequently just as valid as the way in which anyone else sees it. In other words, my own subjectivity alone provides

3. Blake, *A Vision of the Last Judgment*, (Keynes edition, Oxford, 1966), p.617.

the criteria for determining what constitutes reality and what unreality: in my own right and without reference to anyone else or to anything else other than my subjective mental images, I am virtually creator of the universe. And the way is open to all the excesses and aberrations of modern psychology and modern art.[4]

In addition, a purely immaterialist idea of space and time—of extension—is, Milosz maintains, something which, from the purely human point of view, is beyond our understanding and feeling: it cannot orientate us in our actual experiential world. Hence it leaves the Lockeian and Newtonian concept undisplaced on its own level as the model which in fact determines our pragmatic life and thinking. The same applies to the ideas on time and space put forward by Swedenborg: basically Swedenborg accepts the Lockeian concept of space on its own level, that of the natural world. He merely insists that spaces in the spiritual world, although like those on earth, are not fixed and stationary, nor can they be determined by measurement as can those in the natural world. Such a view virtually strengthens the already disastrous dichotomy between the concept of an external reality subject to immutable natural laws which is the sphere of science and the concept of an inner reality of human subjectivity or spiritual vision which is the sphere of religion and whose coordinates, so to speak, have no relationship to the physical world.

Milosz fully acknowledges that, as he puts it, 'the mystics alone have a precise and sane notion of space and time', just as he fully acknowledges that Reality itself is beyond space and time—beyond 'space-time'. He

---

4. Ronald Knox aptly points to the dilemma inherent in this form of idealism in his limerick,

> There once was a man who said, 'God
> Must think it exceedingly odd
>   If he finds that this tree
>   Continues to be
> When there's no one about in the Quad.

And the absurdity of the dilemma itself is rebuked with equal aptness in the anonymous reply,

> Dear Sir, Your astonishment's odd,
> I am always about in the Quad;
>   And that's why this tree
>   Will continue to be,
> Since observed by Yours faithfully, GOD.

recognized as distinctly as Berkeley and Blake that for thought concerned only with sensible objects the question of reality arises only in correlation with those objects. But he regarded it as his task to heal the dichotomy that has bedevilled western thought at least from the time of the Renaissance, by so metamorphosing our idea of the physical universe that the sphere of science should be at one with the sphere of religion and there would be an identity of religious dogma and scientific concept. He believed that only a metaphysician nourished above all on the central verities of the Christian tradition was in a position to carry out such a task, for the simple reason that Christianity possesses at its heart a vision in which, far from there being any opposition between spirit and matter, Creator and Creation, both remain in indivisible unity, however clearly distinct they are in manifestation. Milosz's thought eschews pantheism just as severely as it eschews a devaluation of the physical world in the name of a purely transcendent spiritual or mental world. But it could be said, paraphrasing Blake's words quoted above, that his purpose was to show that the material world has a dwelling-place which is anything but in fallacy and that its existence is anything but an imposture.

To this end, the first step was, as we saw, to dispel the basic error of post-Cartesian physics and to divorce the idea of space from all connection with infinity. Space—the very space that surrounds us—is absolutely alien to any idea of the infinite, just as it is absolutely alien to any idea of the finite. The question of the infinite or of the finite does not arise concerning it. It is not its own container, nor is it the container of other things. It is not even the place in which we are situated as substance. Consequently it cannot be sub-divided or multiplied. And the same applies to time: time is not a category which can be cut into the three slices of past, present and future. It cannot be multiplied to eternity. The infinite and the eternal are qualities that pertain to the non-spatial and non-temporal Reality of the Divine alone. In other words, the whole concept of duration, far from being the greatest achievement of the human mind over the last few centuries, is a false concept and corresponds to nothing in the reality of things.

Yet since this concept itself is a consequence of the idea that the only reliable knowledge we can have about the physical world is that which can be obtained from the application of modern mathematics to sense-data, it follows that, if this concept is false, either the mathematics which determine it are a false mathematics, or they are incapable of providing an adequate knowledge of the physical world, or both simultaneously. In fact—although Milosz does not say this in so many words—since the calculations and demonstrations of modern mathematics presuppose the deployment of an entirely negative and non-existent category and are impossible without deploying it, the knowledge which can be derived from this mathematics can only be a negative—that is to say a non-existent or false—knowledge. I am referring to the use of the symbol o—nothing or nought—understood in a purely privative way, as the total absence of both quality and quantity, which was introduced into European mathematics at the time of the Renaissance. Since there is absolutely no correspondence between this symbol and any reality in the physical universe, to deploy it in attempting to reach conclusions about the nature of this universe is to vitiate one's efforts from the start. No calculation or demonstration involving a false—a non-existent—category of thought can produce anything but an entirely fictitious knowledge of what it purports to explain or describe. As the post-Cartesian concepts of space and time have been determined by a mathematics that does involve such a category, and as without it it is incapable of performing the operations of multiplication and division which actually determine the concepts in question, the concepts themselves must be fictitious. And the same may be said of all other concepts of the physical universe determined by such mathematical procedures. Well may Milosz call modern mathematics the fetish of a barbarous science.

If space-time is entirely alien to any idea of the infinite or the finite, is it therefore illusion? Milosz would reply that it is illusion when envisaged in itself, independent of a context within which it is embraced and apart from which it has no existence whatsoever. In grasping this context, one must realize first of all that the three elements of empirical perception—space, time and matter—constitute a single indivisible concept. Matter, that is to say, is identical with space and time, and we know and can know of no other matter than space and time. The origins of space are thus physical: space is identical with universal matter, a single and perfect body, the notion of which is inseparable from that of time.

But this space, this time, this matter, where are they to be found? The answer is that they are to be found in movement. Space, time and matter, themselves identical, are the elements of a tripartite concept of movement which itself embraces them. This is to say that the trinity of space, time and matter is given to us simultaneously, as a whole, in the unity of movement. Space-time is not the place of movement: space-time is the creation of movement, is the matter of movement. Movement is therefore the generator of space-time-matter. It is the contemporary and synonym of space-time-matter in the actual world.

Manifestation—the physical universe—is thus a movement in which space, time and matter are identical. This movement is one, because it is space and time apprehended in matter. Matter is consequently itself one, like that by virtue of which it is matter—and it is matter by virtue of movement. A single movement is the unalterable matter of space and time. Correspondingly, the idea of diversity exists solely because things are in movement. The sun is a movement we call the sun, the heart is a movement we call the heart, and so it is with everything before our senses, physical and mental. Everything that can be grasped by our senses is pure relationship between moving bodies. Relationship is the fundamental law of all phenomena. Space, *place*, is nothing else than the relation between movement A and movement B. The materiality of space is but the relationships between moving bodies. The cosmos itself is a perfect sphere of movement-space-time-matter whose interior space is a pure relation of these moving bodies.

Total space—the whole physical universe—is therefore real: it is matter itself. Or, to put the same thing the other way round, matter —universal matter—is a single whole forming total space. And this perfect cosmic body—this perfect simultaneity, absolute identity and indivisible unity of space, matter and time—is movement. It is thanks to movement that the cosmos is.

Yet movement, which is matter, space and time, also possesses an anteriority with respect to the other three elements of the fundamental cosmic notion. For space, time and matter are given by movement, and this in spite of the fact that movement is their contemporary and synonym. Hence there is the need to reconcile the priority of movement and its perfect simultaneity with space, time and matter, and such a reconciliation is achieved by positing an initial movement which is antecedant to cosmic movement. For although space is, so to say, subsumed and embraced in cosmic movement, the origin of this movement itself has not yet been identified. Hence the question, 'Where is space', or, more pertinently, 'Where am I?', with which we started, still remains unanswered in any definitive sense, for we still do not know where cosmic movement itself is situated.

This necessity of giving an account of the origin of cosmic movement leads Milosz to his reaffirmation of a Christian metaphysics—a metaphysics that could replace the dynamic concept of sequence proposed by modern science with that of what he calls divine instantaneity. This metaphysics could be described as a metaphysics of light in the sense elaborated by Grosseteste in his works, *De Luce* and the *Hexaemeron*, themselves greatly influenced by the *Hexaemeron* of St Basil the Great and in certain respects by St Augustine, John Scottus Eriugena in his *Periphyseon*, and the mediaeval philosophic school of Chartres which preceded that of Oxford. It also has affinities with the metaphysics of light in Suhravardi's 'oriental theosophy'.

According to this metaphysics, God exteriorizes the non-manifest archetypal world of his thought in an emission or projection of incorporeal light. He exteriorizes it in what Milosz calls the Nothing. This Nothing is not to be confused with the void, still less with the modern mathematical concept of nothing—the nought—which is a purely negative category. On the contrary, this metaphysical Nothing is Nothing (No thing) simply from the point of view of material existence. It designates the absence of space-matter, not the absence of spiritual energy.

The incorporeal Fire, then, projects its incorporeal light upon the Nothing, upon that which is not a place but simply the idea—the idea-archetype—of an exterior. This is the original *Fiat Lux*; and through it all the ideas of creation (including the idea-archetype of the exterior or Nothing upon which the incorporeal light is projected) are made manifest uncreatedly in this light. The incorporal light is as it were an image of the non-manifest Divine occulted in Its indivisible Unity. Simultaneously, it is the archetypal world prior to manifestation in the physical universe, the place in which everything that is created is contained. It thus constitutes a link, an intermediary plane between the Universe-archetype as thought by the Divine and the world of created manifestation. It is a kind of stage where all things happen in instantaneity, simultaneity. In other words, it constitutes what Henry Corbin was to call, some quarter of a century later, the *mundus imaginalis*, and which we will designate in the next chapter as the world of divine Wisdom.

This original *Fiat Lux* by means of which God as inconceivable fire transmutes himself into incorporeal light—a transmutation synonymous, Milosz tell us, with that by means of which God as Law transmutes Himself into the God of universal sacrifice and inexpressible love and beauty—is succeeded, not temporally but in terms of instantaneous and contemporaneous succession, by the metamorphosis or transmutation of incorporeal light itself into physical light. In instantaneity God 'exteriorizes' Himself in non-corporeal light, and in the same instantaneity does non-corporeal light create physical light, the clothing of the universe in its form of beauty and bride. This is the creation *ex nihilo*, out of the Nothing-Universe of incorporeal light: a Nothing which is not a negative category but the plenitude of divine uncreated energies.

The origin of cosmic movement, therefore, lies in incorporeal light itself. The initial movement antecedent to cosmic movement is that imparted to physical light through the transmutation of incorporeal light into physical light whose expansion creates the universe of manifested matter. But physical light is but a more rarified and subtle form of blood, in that blood, too, is a transmutation of incorporeal light—a transmutation exemplified in every eucharistic celebration. Thus together physical light and blood constitute the living cosmic matter endowed with movement and may be said to correspond to the vital spirit—quicksilver—of the alchemists or to the Hindu *prāna* or to the *Orenda* of the North American Indians. Contemporaneous with the original *Fiat Lux*, this cosmic matter—blood and light—is the sum of the spiritual energies manifested in creation; it is the beauty and love of God manifest uncreatedly in immaterial light transmuted into a single movement. The first mover, it teaches us how to situate all spatial things in movement alone and all temporal things in instantaneity alone, allowing us to perceive how everything that was, is and will be happens in the same single instant.

This single movement which is the transmutation of incorporeal light is, therefore, the unalterable matter of space and time. It is not the inconceivable passage from one place to another place, but the intelligible metamorphosis from a state to a state. The entire secret of manifestation—of creation—resides in the transmission through blood and light, living cosmic matter, of a movement in which space, matter and time are identical. Blood, the essence of movement and universal rhythm, is the container, the foundation, the *place*, of the simultaneity and instantaneity of these three basic elements of the cosmic notion. They are enclosed within the unfathomable but tangible unity which blood—our inner movement—emits and projects.

For the source of blood is the indivisible unity; and yet, by virtue of instantaneity, blood is also this unity itself. At the same time, blood takes us into the tripartite world. Spiritual light, by becoming the movement of physical light, also produces the movement of blood, and this movement generates space-time-matter. The whole universe runs in us: it is our blood. Our blood is the *fiat* that, even before the cosmic blossoming, received the first imprint of movement for the sole purpose of clothing with a physical container the indivisible concept of matter-space-time. Space, time and matter are given in the instantaneity not only of knowledge but also of simple awareness by universal movement, which is the *fiat*, that is the projection of our blood beyond its original unity. Yet, again by virtue of instantaneity, this cosmic blood is still in the impetus of the first emission by means of which God projects incorporeal light: it perpetuates this first emission and is simultaneous with it. Hence light—the spiritual light produced by this original emission—is the soul in our blood. And since this blood is the creator of organic space-time-matter, the soul of the physical universe is also spiritual light.

The place of man, therefore, as well as of the physical universe in its entirety—their 'where'—is a spiritual place: neither man nor the physical universe has a *physical* situation, and the idea that they do have a *physical* situation is the original error of thought that alienates man from his true place and casts him out into the wilderness. A creation of God's incorporeal light, man and the finite universe can be situated only in this light, and *they can be situated nowhere else*, however much we may pretend that they can be.

Moreover, as this light is the knowledge that God has of Himself—the projection of the non-manifest archetypal world of His thought in a vision of love and beauty—to say that man and the finite universe are situated in it, and are only situated there, is to say that they really exist only in the spiritual vision of the Creator. The universe—created space-matter—is a vision of beauty and love seen by the only Seer. My only place is in the One who has breathed into the Nothing the ecstatic mirage of the world's beauty.

Yet at the same time this vision—this knowledge that God has of himself—is identical with what is deepest and purest in our own being. It is the infinite within. I am a heartbeat of God, a pulsation of divine love. If I am to find my true place—to be where I truly belong—I can only do so consequently in a gravitation which is that of this love. This love is our only true reality and when it transports us into the incorporeal light which it makes visible, the whole universe is restored to its place, a place determined by the relation of this light to the divine hidden fire. As we said above, however much Creator and Creation are distinct in manifestation—there is no question of any pantheism—they are none the less an indivisible unity in spirit. The world, material in appearance, is a spiritual vision of the Divine: it is situated in the incorporeal Light that is synonymous with the *mundus imaginalis* or the world of Sophia aeterna—and woe to those, Milosz adds, who make of it a monstrous material deity extended to infinity or situated in an absurd void without end.

The whole history of mankind since the fall, Milosz maintains, has been in essence a battle between the idea of infinite eternal matter on the one hand and that of the incorporeal light on the other. Straining to embrace a universe of which matter itself is the place, we displace ourselves from this light and exchange the infinite within ourselves for a space without end, the eternally fleeing product of ceaseless multiplication in which there is room for anything except for place. The ideas of multiplying and of extending are the true origin of all the misfortunes of mankind and nature. And what finally is the concept of the black hole which so preoccupies modern scientists but the projection, on to the so-called external world, of the black hole—the 'soul-shuddering vacuum'—which man opens in his consciousness when he commits his original act of apostasy, alienates himself from the light, and plunges into the void of spiritual darkness and self-oblivion?

This, then, is the vision of the cosmos with which Milosz presents us and which he hoped would, in due course, supplant the materialist interpretations of the physical universe—indeed, which he believed *must* supplant these interpretations if we are to escape from the infernal world into which our denial of the uncreated spiritual universe—the Nothing-universe—has plunged us and in which, as he puts it, we suffer endlessly from the torment of being in God and of not knowing it. Naturally, in a *résumé* such as this it is impossible to do more than to outline the bare contours of the vision. It is not possible to convey the richness, warmth, colour and sheer poetry with which Milosz himself clothes these contours. It is not possible to convey his profound articulation of such themes as the feminine principle of manifestation, or the nature of man and woman, or the redemptive power of beauty, or to give a sense of the deep compassion for man as for all creatures with which his writings are imbued. To experience these qualities one must read and re-read his own works.

Milosz was anything but an abstract impersonal philosopher. He considered that all thought, all art, all science not generated out of love and prayer, and not baptised and confirmed in inner experience, was a defamation of life and intelligence, however impressive it might appear.

His own later poetry, as well as his metaphysical works, were born out of year after year of persistent struggle, suffering, loneliness and study, to be consummated finally in a mystical transport in which the last veils of illusion were torn away and he was granted the vision of the universe, divine, human and physical, in all its magnificence, beauty and love. This is why they are impregnated with the kind of authority and incontravertible authenticity which one finds only in scripture and sacred art.

At the same time, in adopting religious and pre-eminently Christian criteria in order to interpret the meaning of his visionary experience, Milosz was in no way doctrinaire. He acknowledges that the truth is one and that some respect and love are enough to discover it in the depths of our consciousness. For him there are but two kinds of people: the negators who profess irreconcilable systems and the modest affirmers who all say the same thing to anyone who knows how to listen. He specifies among his spiritual ancestors 'modest affirmers' like Pythagoras and the Pre-Socratics, Plato, the initiates of Alexandria, the Neoplatonists of the Middle Ages, the Christian mystics, and later adepts like Paracelsus, Goethe and Claude de Saint Martin. Tireless reader of the Bible—his knowledge of Hebrew gave him direct access to the Old Testament—his early studies had initiated him into the world of Egyptology and of the pre-Greek and pre-Roman civilizations of the Near East. Though he regarded the Reformation and Protestantism in general as a total disaster, he was fully capable of learning deeply from such Protestant writers as Boehme, Swedenborg and Goethe. Far be it from him, he wrote, to judge the good Jew, the good Muslim, the good Buddhist.

None the less, it is as a committed and practising Christian—a Catholic Christian—that Milosz finally speaks, and we have already noted how he insisted that his own teachings were in complete accord with those of traditional Christian doctrine. His metaphysics, he affirmed, were a Christian metaphysics, and his mission an annunciation of future Christianity. He maintained that any rational proposition which does not conform to the teachings of Christian doctrine can only be, even when based upon the most rigorous mathematical and physical evidence, an illusion of our senses and of our tiny and arrogant insect mind. His aspiration was to prepare for the reconciliation of Christian doctrine and the concepts of science—not of course of our infamous and blind contemporary science which, he states, is powerless where anything is concerned that is not lucre or murder, but of true science, the passionate and loving science of the Divine. Without such a reconciliation, he maintained, there could be no spiritual or artistic regeneration, no reborn humanity

It was because of this that he considered that the greatest spiritual task which confronts us today is to metamorphose the modern scientific concept of the physical universe from within, because, for reasons that we have explained above, such a metamorphosis is the *sine qua non* of this reconciliation and hence itself the precondition of any genuine revival of human life on earth, of any genuine restoration of a sacramental relationship between ourselves and the world we live in. If Milosz is right, then the challenge which he presents to those of us who claim that we, too, aspire to such a revival and restoration—to the recovery of the sense of the sacred reality of our own lives as well as of the life of everything else that exists—is too obvious to need stating; and we do Milosz scant honour if, while acknowledging him to be a significant, even a major intellectual figure, we yet at the same time refuse to confront it.

7 Notes Towards the Restitution of Sacred Cosmology

IN THE INTRODUCTION I said that the task we faced was twofold: first, to describe as clearly as possible the kind of self-image and world-view which have landed us in our present plight; and, second, to attempt to recover, or rediscover, the vision of man and nature—or what I called the theoanthropocosmic vision—which would make it possible for us to perceive and hence to experience both ourselves and the world we live in as the sacred realities that they are. And I added that this meant that we have to establish in our minds a clear picture of how and why these realities are sacred, and even sacramental, since just to assert that they are so in an arbitrary manner could well be only a form of sentimentalism.

What is required—though this may sound somewhat formidable and forbidding—is a kind of mystical-intellectual knowledge of God and divine realities that is not confined to the subjective inwardness of personal experience and that can be translated into a knowledge of the world and of the cosmos that illuminates every object and every form of being. In this way what may begin as an interior and even other-wordly experience of spiritual realities is extended to embrace the whole cosmos, and to provide the life-blood of an integral cosmological vision.

In the last chapter, through the writings of Oskar Milosz, I took the first step in trying to re-establish the essential lineaments of this vision. In this final chapter I will attempt to consolidate more fully what was there affirmed, formulating the vision now in the personalized terms of the sacred mythology of the Christian tradition.

As noted above,[1] by and large we have not been well served in this respect by Christian theology. It got off to a bad start. Already in St Paul's epistles there are warnings about the elemental spirits of the world,[2] and the idea that God is present in the elements—in water, springs, stars, trees and everything else—is more than discouraged by the Apostolic Church. It is true that, as we saw in the opening chapter of this book, a few theologians from these early centuries—St Justin Martyr, St Irenaeus, St Clement of Alexandria, Origen—do proclaim a vision in which the main Christian doctrines—the Trinity, Creation, Incarnation—are seen as interrelated, the one supporting and illuminating the other; and this synthesizing rather than divisive theology does give a positive cosmological content to what is meant when St Paul, for instance, speaks of Christ as being born prior to all creation.[3]

Yet only too soon is this synthesis disrupted. The links between the doctrines of the Trinity, the Incarnation and Creation are broken, and increasingly theology is split into watertight compartments. Attempts are made, for instance, to form a theology of the Trinity that is concerned solely with the interior interrelationships of the three Persons and that has no reference whatsoever either to the Incarnation or to Creation. Similarly, Christology—the question of the two natures in Christ, of how Christ's manhood is linked to His Godhead—also becomes an end in itself. And although solutions are given to these questions, at the Councils of Nicaea (325) and Chalcedon (451), the solutions remain abstract.

For where there is no longer an understanding of how one member of the Trinity—the Incarnate Logos—is also manifestation, is also creation, or of how the inner relations of Godhead and manhood in Christ are the same as those effective between God and the world, there can never be a full vision, dynamic and organic, of who God is, or man is, or creation is, let alone of what these doctrines should mean for us personally, in purely practical terms. The Christological problem—which is also the anthropological problem—and the cosmological problem are interwoven with and inseparable from the Trinitarian problem, and if we split them apart we end up with the kind of systematic, analytical view of Christianity that characterizes mediaeval scholasticism, or with the kind of disincarnate cosmology that marks, for instance, the natural science of St Gregory

---

1. See chap. 1 above. 2. cf. Col. 2:8. 3. cf. Col. I:15–16.

Palamas, which reiterates the depressive notion that all phenomena other than human are soulless (*apsycha*) and mindless or irrational (*aloga*).[4] To fail to relate creation to the Incarnation, and to fail to relate both to the Trinity, is to mutilate its mystery at its heart, and this is the same as saying that it is to mutilate the mystery of our own lives at its heart.

The loss of the theoanthropocosmic vision hinted at by the early theologians I mentioned[5] is in fact most evident—especially in relation to our theme—precisely in the loss of the cosmic significance of the Incarnation. What this significance presupposes is that as well as and independently of the historical and individual manifestation of the Son of God in Jesus of Nazareth, the Logos already knows, and continues to know, manifestation and materialization in the cosmos as a whole, in both man and nature. This is to say that there is the cosmic Sonship of the divine Logos as appearing in the world of creation, and there is Sonship revealed in the individual and historical Jesus. The historical appearance of Christ is only one form of embodiment; the universe of matter is another form, and in this form the cosmic Christ is from the beginning and always showing forth images of God in nature, for nature is the Body of God.

The doctrine of the God-man, therefore, refers not simply to the historical Incarnation of the God-man Himself; it refers also and equally to the theandric union between God and the whole created world, through man and in man. The Son is generated—and eternally generated—'prior to all creation'; but in and through that generation the created aspect of the world appears as an immediate and inseparable consequence. The cosmogonic problem is linked with the generation of the Logos. Creation is an eternal act which from the side of God, so to speak, is above time altogether, since it pertains to the eternal act of generation of the Logos; but some of the effects of this eternal act of generation are manifest in a temporal and spatial form, and these effects constitute what we call creation. These two aspects of a single divine act—the generative and the cosmogonic—are clearly distinct, for the second depends on the first, and not *vice versa*; but they are also linked and inseparable.

---

4. See St Gregory Palamas, *The One Hundred and Fifty Chapters*, ed. and trs. Robert E. Sinkewicz (Toronto, 1988), 3,4,8,25,26,31 et al.

5. See chap. 1 above, pp.27–29, for the hint of this vision given by these theologians.

It is this cosmic significance of the Incarnation that has been eclipsed,[6] so much so that Incarnation is now almost exclusively identified with the historical manifestation of the Son at Bethlehem. The Trinity is meant to be the ground and pattern of all living things, but how this is so remains unexplained because the Trinitarian doctrine of the eternal generation of the Son as the true Image of the Father is divorced from the doctrine of creation, and hence it can no longer be seen in what sense or how all nature perpetually also shows forth true images of the Father. Cosmology is divorced both from Trinitarian doctrine and from Christology. The result is a view that separates God from man and the world by a virtually unbridgeable gulf.

We are left with a kind of either-or position and must choose either God or the world; and this in its turn issues either in a kind of Protestant a-cosmism or even in the anti-cosmism of pseudo-asceticism—an asceticism closed to the sacral sense of sensible beauty and out of hostility or cowardice accusing those possessing this sense of the 'crime' of aestheticism; or it issues in a view that accepts the world at its face value and that rapidly degenerates into the secularization of life with which we are only too familiar. Indeed, one could say that it was the virtual cosmological vacuum fostered by so much Christian theology that provided the opportunity for the success of that non-Christian and ultimately totally profane view of things which we described in chapters two and three above.

What has happened is that a kind of irreducible dualism has crept into Christian theology. God and creation—and, correspondingly, the order of salvation and the order of nature—are seen as irreducibly two. There is still of course a doctrine of creation, but increasingly this takes the form of regarding creation as coming originally from God but after that as enjoying full independent existence, to such an extent that it is considered to constitute an entity entirely on its own and to be virtually autonomous. The old Aristotelian spectre of 'man in a state of pure nature' again raises its head. Such dualism sees creation as a movement *ad extra*, as God creating something outside Himself, another than Himself, a second subject of Being. God is set over against creation, and in

6. Though recollections of it lingered on even in western Christian iconography at least down to the thirteenth century, for they are evident in such mediaeval world-maps as Hereford Cathedral's Mappa Mundi: see Cecilia Twinch, 'To be heard, read and seen', in *Beshara*, issue 12, pp. 24–27.

particular against man. The encounter between God and man is envisaged not as an encounter between the individual human being and a
spiritual presence that is the true personal subject of that being. It is
envisaged as an encounter between the individual human and an inaccessible, transcendent, non-individuated God. My human existence is felt to
be not so much the existentiation of the Divine but as something added *ad
extra*, as a kind of adjunct, to the Divine.

As a result man feels himself to be at the mercy of a single undifferentiated omnipotence from which all men are equidistant. He is lost in a
religious or social collectivity, or religio-socio collectivity, which, rather
than trying to unite each person with his own spiritual essence, attempts
to impose a kind of abstract, totalitarian, unilateral monotheism upon
everyone. Having lost his direct link with his own spiritual essence and
archetype, his own personal *logos* and *sophia*—and this is tantamount to
having lost his knowledge of himself—each individual is exposed to a
hypotrophy that can easily degenerate into spiritual imperialism. Again,
we are thrust into a kind of either-or position: either we are forced to
affirm things without perceiving their transcendent dimension; or we
divorce that transcendence from the things through which alone it is
manifest. We separate religion from aesthetics, the experience of the
Divine from the experience in sensible objects of their primal and eternal
beauty.

Perhaps never before have we been faced so urgently with the question
of the significance of creation and of man's role in creation; with the need
to justify the world in God, to see how the creaturely world is united with
the divine world, religion with aesthetics. We have to attempt the
reconquest of the idea that God is not only the Creator of the world but
that He is also in some sense what He creates. A true doctrine of creation
must start with the affirmation that any conception of the creature as a
second being existing apart from God is a false doctrine. Creatures not
only take their being from God but are kept in being by remaining in
God. They are in God's Being: 'In Him we live, we move and have our
being.'[7] To create does not mean giving independent existence to
another—does not mean that the creature can be or subsist on its own.
Creation as an act from the side of God is not the making of a second
outside God, who is the First. Creation takes place within God, not
outside God. It is the rise of 'otherness' in God, of a new order, the order

7. Acts 17:28.

of manifestation, not the establishing of 'another' with an independent existence. It is in God that the world exists, for 'of Him, and through Him, and to Him, are all things.'[8]

In this idea of God creating the universe within Himself there is no separation between God and creation that is capable of growing into an unbridgeable gulf. It is God's own creative power that existentiates all the forms and receptacles that constitute the revealed and manifest dimension of His Being. Creation is nothing less than the manifestation of God's hidden Being: the other world is this world, this world is the other world. If the kingdom of God can come on earth it is because in essence the earth is the kingdom of God. The path to knowledge and rebirth does not consist in denying and doing away with the manifest world; it consists in recognizing it for what it is and in esteeming it for what it is: not a reality beside and in addition to essential divine reality, but precisely a revelation of this divine reality. To recognize the manifest world in this way is to be delivered from the fiction that it constitutes an autonomous datum, from the belief that it is simply a material, objective object. It is to realize that there is no value in a material fact except in so far as through it we perceive its immaterial reality—the transcendent meaning or spiritual presence—that it manifests and enshrines.

The only science of nature worthy of the title is one that induces an understanding of the reality of this divine presence of which each sensible form is the revelation or epiphany. It is one that helps us to discover not what obscure or unconscious force produces things, but what divine thought, or image, or idea, unfolding in the spiritual world, is at work in each of them. It is to know why the opening of a flower is a form of divine resurrection. Each sensible thing has its own personal *logos* and *sophia* by which it is constituted, and it is this *logos* and *sophia* whose perfection is individuated in each object of the senses or the intellect.

The invisible spiritual presence and the visible form of this presence constitute an indissoluble unity, or bi-unity. This does not mean that they are existentially identical: existentially the invisible spiritual presence is not the visible form, and *vice versa*. But they are reciprocal and complementary. There is no opposition between God and created things, there is synergy and reciprocity. Each thing possesses the capacity to move from an imperfect harmony with God (and hence with itself) to a perfect harmony, the perfect harmony being achieved when the personal

8. Rom. 3:36.

logos and *sophia* of each created being is the effective and determinative subject of that being. There is no evolution or surpassing of the created order; there is only the realization by each being of the symmetry and divinity bestowed on it by God.

In this perspective, then, the sensible world is the image, the icon of the celestial world, and enshrines the spiritual reality of which it is the image: the two interpenetrate. Everything organic hangs together, coheres, is symbiotic, and each element of a true synthesis is made whole and perfect to the degree to which it integrates itself with the whole, with the world of spiritual essences or archetypes in whose image it is created. Nothing less than this mutual inherence and coherence—than this interpenetration—is adequate to explain the real self of each created thing, for this is the true setting of each created thing. To abstract something from its setting, and to treat it as though it existed independently of its setting, is to murder it at its roots, in thought if not in deed.

The main obstacles to overcoming the dualistic conception of things that has crept into Christian theology—this idea that God creates the world as something exterior to Himself—would seem to be four. With one exception they tend to take the form of half truths that are asserted as if they were whole truths. In this way they exclude their contraries, which equally are half truths but which, blended with the assertions they appear to contradict, allow these assertions to be seen as the half truths they are. The first such assertion is that God creates the world out of nothing, *ex nihilo*. What this statement would appear to be guarding against is the idea that there is some kind of pre-existing, independent material substratum out of which God creates, an idea that would immediately introduce another form of dualism by positing the existence of something totally outside God at the basis of creation. But applied literally and rigorously in the way it usually is, it defeats its own purpose; for it then establishes itself, or is established, as if it were positing a *nihil*—a nothing—that is totally outside God, that represents a total voidance and deficiency of God. As a consequence it introduces a dualism similar to that which it was intended to guard against.

For no manner of thought can bridge the gap between Creator and creature if creation itself is conceived as *creatio ex nihilo* in which the *nihil* in question is regarded as something outside God and as something totally deprived and deficient of God, a kind of pure deficiency. Such a category is beyond conception—in fact, it is impossible for there to be such a category—and hence to posit it at the root of creation is to posit in creation itself a dimension that is inconceivable and ultimately totally unreal. A being that has issued out of something that is totally unreal must by definition be eternally distinct and separate from God. There must always be opposition and distance between them. One discovers the mystery of being in the experience of one's own being. If one thinks of oneself as a created entity drawn from a nothingness that is set over against an all-powerful Uncreated Being, how can one make this discovery, for what possible relationship can there be between such nothingness and God? There cannot even be coherent thought about a non-existent category, a category of pure illusion. In any case, as John Scottus Eriugena pointed out, there can be no privation of relationship before relationship exists, and no negation of existence before existence.[9]

The doctrine of creation *ex nihilo*, as it is usually understood and applied, is not Christian, however much it may have entered into Christian theology. There is no *ex* at all where being is concerned: even the word 'existing' is itself misleading, for strictly speaking nothing really leaves that in which it is rooted, no being leaves Being. If the phrase, *ex nihilo*, is to have any significance beyond that of guarding against the idea that God creates out of some self-subsisting, independent element, the 'nothing' in question cannot indicate a purely negative category; on the contrary, it must indicate either the metaphysical Nothing of which Milosz speaks, a world of uncreated spiritual energies in which there is no thing; or, beyond that, beyond even Being itself, a world of pure potentiality, the *Ungrund* or Abyss in which the unmanifest virtualities or divine Names of God Himself are occluded.[10]

9. For Eriugena's understanding of the meaning of *ex nihilo* in this context, see Dermot Moran, *The Philosophy of John Scottus Eriugena* (Cambridge, 1989), chap. 12, *passim*.

10. Already in the fourth century the Cappadocian theologians recognize that *non-being* is one of the Names of God. St Gregory of Nyssa, for example, identifies the *nihil* out of which this world is created with God Himself in His superessential Non-being (see H.A. Wolfson, 'The identification of *ex nihilo* with Emanation in Gregory of Nyssa', reprinted in his *Studies in the History of Philosophy and Religion* (Cambridge, Mass., 1973), pp.199–221). Creation *ex nihilo* means God's own self-creation, His self-manifestation in theophanies, His movement from darkness to light. Nothing (*nihil*), Eriugena remarks, is another name for God, and creation *ex nihilo* is creation from or out of God (see Dermot Moran, *The Philosophy of John Scottus Eriugena*, op. cit, pp.236 and 238ff.).

As Jacob Boehme was to put it: 'God created the world out of nothing because He Himself dwells in nothing—that is, He dwells in Himself.'[11]

The second obstacle is a hopelessly misbegotten notion of time and space. Time and space in themselves have no objective or independent existence. Neither is an objective milieu, or an entity in itself. They are simply qualitative aspects, and two aspects only, of creation, and, like materiality, they arise only as the epiphenomena of the divine creative act itself. They are qualities that result when material modalities of creation are related and compared to other modalities; and they cease to exist when creation is seen as a whole in relation to the Creator.

It is this understanding of time and space that has been increasingly eroded, and what has been put in its place is a notion which, although it is as old at least as Arianism, received its definitive and most totally misconceived formulation in Newton's thought—indeed, his whole physics, like that of so many of his successors, is entirely dependent on it, and this in spite of the fact that such a notion is beyond every form of experimental verification and can never be anything but pure *a priori* hypothesis.

What this notion asserts is that time and space are realities in themselves; that they are absolute, true and ultimately mathematical; and that they constitute infinite, homogeneous entities entirely independent of material objects, motions and even human knowledge altogether. Time flows equally from eternity to eternity; space exists all at once in infinite immovability; and it is into both that creatures are plunged as into some vast pre-existing containers. Such a notion of time and space inevitably involves envisaging man apart from God, creation apart from God; for if what is created has its existence in an extended time-space continuum which, even though it may initially have been created by God, is now independent of Him and virtually autonomous, clearly there can be no actual and effective interpenetration of the divine and the human, of the divine and what is spatial and temporal.[12]

The third obstacle takes the form not so much of an assertion as of a rejection—the rejection of what is called pantheism. Such a rejection is perfectly justified in so far as it is directed against the error of confounding God and creation—of worshipping creation rather than the Creator. For in what could the creatureliness of creation consist if

11. See his *Psychologia Verum*, Question 7.23.
12. For a fuller account of this notion of time and space, see chap. 3 above.

creation is the same as or identical or one subject with God? Yet pantheism itself is right in insisting that creation does not constitute a second subject of Being, something that is outside God and independent of Him, an entity entirely on its own. And the rejection of pantheism *tout court* generally implies also a rejection of the truth of this insistence contained within it. For there is no 'another' to God: God is not 'another' to the world, creation is not 'another' to God, and in no way can it be an entity on its own account, existing outside God.

None the less, if pantheism is right in refusing to see creation as a movement whereby God creates something outside Himself, and in insisting that it is rooted in God, this still leaves unanswered the problem of how, if God is the sole subject of existence, all particulars—all that we experience as concrete beings—can be rooted in God without being identical or one subject with Him. How can they be plural manifestations or appearances of their single root? How can they be immanent in God without God losing His transcendence with respect to them and without destroying His oneness? If a transcendent God without the correlative of an immanent creation makes an idol of creation by positing it as a separate existence outside God, how can insistence on the immanence of creation in God not issue in pantheism and hence deprive the creature as such of all eternal identity and significance? It is these questions that we have to answer, for otherwise we will be forced either into some form of pantheism, or into the dualism of a theology that would have creation to be an act whereby God creates something that is external to His own Being.

The fourth obstacle in the way of overcoming such a dualism is the assertion that God creates entirely out of His own free will and not under the compulsion of any necessity. This again is a defensive assertion. It is meant to guard against the idea that God is under constraint to create because there is something more powerful than God which compels Him to do so; for if this were the case, then this 'something' would be God. Hence there is absolutely no necessity involved in God's creation of the world: it is a free expression of His will and He could quite as well have chosen not to create it as to create it.

This argument again forces on its proponents the notion that God in creating creates something exterior to Himself. For if creation could equally well not be as be, it means that it is in no way necessary to God's self-fulfilment: He could equally well be what He is without creating. But what is not a necessary aspect or consequence of God being what He is is something adventitious, gratuitous and even a kind of appendage. And what is adventitious, gratuitous and a kind of appendage must be exterior to God. Hence creation is seen as a movement *ad extra* where God is concerned, and the dualism is endorsed.

Once again we are dealing with a half truth that tries to usurp the rank of a whole truth. For freedom may be liberty of choice and an independence from external constraint. But it is by no means only that. For there is a higher form of freedom, a paradoxical 'determinative' freedom, which is not merely a liberty of choice. This freedom which is attained in apparent determinism is not a negative indeterminacy—the feeling that 'I can do it or I need not do it', or that 'I could do it if I wanted to'; it is a positive natural spontaneity. Non-compulsion from without may be one form of freedom; but compulsion from within is another and higher form. And it is this kind of compulsion that God is under when He creates.

The creative act has its adequate and sufficient ground in God's Being, and so is an essential and necessary self-determination of that Being: that God creates the world means that He could not not create it. The divine creative act belongs to the fulness of divine life, without any mechanical necessity or outer compulsion. God, with power to create, could not not be a Creator. God is love, and God 'so loved the world'. The reality of love is a property inherent in the essence of the lover. It is not an accident or an incident or something ancillary: it is the very colour and texture of the lover's being. The divine Lover—God—cannot not love at all, or love to a limited extent, or not extend His love to the farthest limits of possibility and so abstain from loving fully. He does not have that choice.

It is the same with His creative power. He does not possess the possibility of not creating or of abstaining from creation. Just as love is as necessary as His own Being since it inheres in that Being, so creation is as necessary as His own Being, for it, too, inheres in it. Creation of the world is not a gratuitous extra. It is the expression of divine life with all the power of necessity, with all the absolute freedom and spontaneity of God's Being. God *qua* God is Creator and Creator *qua* Creator is God: creation is intrinsic to His very life, it is the inner landscape of His own Being, God making Himself visible to Himself and simultaneously making Himself visible to us. It is in some sense His very self. [13]

13. Implicit in this understanding of things is also the conclusion, touched on in chapter one above, that it is impossible to conceive of a time in which God's creativity

Creation, then, is God making Himself visible, or knowable, to Himself. It is God revealing Himself to Himself. That is the initial motive of creation: the desire of God to reveal Himself and to know Himself in beings through being known by them. Being, or Mind, as a subject, issues from its own formless, unmanifest state in order to possess a means whereby it can know its own subjectivity, as a mirror in which it sees its own face. It is the desire of the God who is 'beyond being', 'who is not'—the *theos agnostos*—unknown and unaffirmed, not only to know Himself and to affirm Himself, but also to be known and affirmed. What we are talking about here is not a process of emanation in the Neoplatonic sense. What is in question is what one might call grades of revelation, or a process whereby God establishes within Himself a descending hierarchy each level of which represents not only a further stage of differentiation but also an increasing degree of subordination and concretization.

Three main degrees or phases in this process of self-revelation may be distinguished. The first is that phase whereby the unknown God reveals Himself to Himself in making Himself conscious of the latent potentialities of His own Being. The second is that whereby this ideal, impersonal, formless and abstract content of the divine Intelligence—of the divine Logos—is differentiated in specific individuated forms, forms possessing a figure, a pattern, a body, although this is still in an immaterial state. These forms constitute the world of the uncreated spiritual energies, of the divine Images or Ideas or of what—since they represent differentiation within the Logos—Christian authors often refer to as *logoi* and

---

is not engaged and in which therefore He is not present and immanent in the activities and creatures through which He manifests Himself. In effect, to say that the world has a beginning in the chronological sense involves two further propositions: first, that there was a time when the world did not exist; and, second, that prior to creating the world God either did not possess any creative power or refrained from using it. But both these propositions are nonsensical, for both presuppose a temporal dimension where none exists: for there is no time prior to the creation of the world and consequently there could not have been a time when the world did not exist; and there is no time *in divinis* such that the words, 'before' and 'after', can be applied to it, and consequently there cannot have been a time prior to which God did not exercise His creative power. We see creation as a temporal act with a beginning in time merely because that corresponds to the restricted mode within which we view things. In reality, since God is not separate from His acts, the act of creation must be an eternal and timeless manifestation of God's eternal and timeless Being. Creation, that is to say, is not an adjunct to God, but is eternal in Him; and all things are consequently in their essence eternal because creation is an eternal aspect of the divine nature.

which we for the rest of this chapter will designate as Image-archetypes, since they are the divine archetypes of everything that exists in the visible and sensible world.[14] This world of the Image-archetypes is an intermediary world between the world of pure formless intelligible realities and the visible world. And the third phase in this theophanic process is that whereby these Image-archetypes manifest themselves in the forms of particular, individuated concrete beings.

What it is important to emphasize is that though each phase or degree in this process is distinct, each is inseparable from the other two; and that though here they are presented as successive phases, yet they all occur in total simultaneity, in divine instantaneousness. There is no question of any lapse or hiatus between them, whether spatial or temporal, for they occur prior to space and time, even though some of their effects have a spatial or temporal character. The three are simply phases or 'moments' in a single divine act through which God reveals Himself to Himself through all eternity.

The first phase—that whereby God becomes conscious of His own latent Intelligence-content—is accomplished in the world of ultimate mystery. This in Christian terms is the world of the Trinity, the world of the three Persons, or hypostases, of God, and of the relations between them; and the theophany that is there accomplished is that through which the potentialities and virtualities concealed in the unknownness of the Father are emancipated from this unknownness in the divine Logos, the Image of the Father. If creation is God's self-revelation, it follows that in Himself—in the totally unmanifest depths of His Being—inhere the potentialities of everything in which when manifest He sees and recognizes Himself. These potentialities are His divine Names; and although these Names cannot be said to be identical with the Godhead, they are not different from it, since they denote what are present in the Godhead from all eternity. And because the name is identical with the thing named, the multiple divine Names are God Himself, and He is one.[15]

14. For the doctrine of the divine *logoi,* see, e.g., St Maximos the Confessor, especially P.G.91, 1329 ABC. A summary of St Maximos's doctrine in this respect, with references to specific texts, is to be found in Lars Thunberg's *Microcosm and Mediator* (Lund, 1965), pp.76–99. See also St Dionysios the Areopagite, *The Divine Names,* P.G.3, 824C.

15. In the Christian tradition the doctrine of the divine Names is chiefly associated with St Dionysios the Areopagite. See above all his treatise, *The Divine Names.* A recent translation of this text into English is to be found in *Pseudo-Dionysius: The*

In eternity—in pre-eternity—before God brought us into existence, we are beings embraced by Him, in His Being; and our own beings are individuations of His Being—of the states and potentialities of God. We appear in Him. We are not simply *with* Him, because we are His very

---

Complete Works, trs. by Colm Luibheid (London, 1987), in the series The Classics of Western Spirituality. In the perspective of this doctrine, God in His ultimate nature might be described as Universal or Supreme Consciousness, and on that level He does not distinguish Himself from us or from anything else; for were we or anything else on that level we would be wholly transformed into Him. It is from our lower plane of finite being that we distinguish between ourselves and Him. It is because of the limitations of our own consciousness that we perceive such a distinction. Yet in another sense in His ultimate nature God is not conscious at all, for consciousness implies a state in which the conscious subject is aware of himself and so becomes the object of his own perception; and such a state is impossible in the ultimate nature of the Godhead: there, there can be no distinction between conscious subject and the object of consciousness. In fact, there cannot be any distinction at all at this level: the ultimate nature of the Godhead is totally undifferentiated.

Yet if this ultimate unity lies behind, or above, all the manifest diversities of this world, it must contain these diversities in itself in an undifferentiated condition. At the same time, if these diversities are to come into existence at all, it must contain in itself in an undifferentiated state the principle of differentiation which from our level allows us to distinguish between ultimate unity and the whole of plurality. This principle of differentiation is thus contained transcendentally in the Godhead itself, and it is this principle that impels the undifferentiated and unrelated Deity to an eternal act of self-manifestation through which He becomes differentiated and related. The Godhead thus possesses two aspects: that which is beyond all differentiation and relationship, and that which embraces a sphere of differentiation and relationship.

It is this latter aspect which constitutes the realm of Being, and it is in this realm that the potentialities not only of creation but also of revelation are first manifest, fused and yet distinct, in the multiple Names of God, and even in the Name, God, itself. Some of these Names are as it were titles of that aspect of the Godhead which is beyond differentiation and relationship or, better stated, they are symbols of this aspect, enshrining as such that of which they are the symbols; and however inadequately they may express its incomprehensible nature, they apply to this nature as a whole and not to any particular element, function or activity in it. But other Names do connote, not the same undifferentiated Deity, but certain differentiated elements, functions or activities. Of these the Names of the three Persons, or hypostases, of the Trinity have preeminence. But also included among these latter Names are those of all particular things whose destiny it is to proceed beyond the sphere of eternity and into the spatial and temporal world of finite creaturely existence. That is why the ultimate identity of every created being is timeless and eternal, and why every created being is potentially divine.

own Being, the Being that He is. We are His organs, the individuations of His Names. The divine Name creates my being, and reciprocally my being posits it in the very same act as that in which it posits me. Yet at the same time our action of positing God is really God positing Himself in us: it is not ourselves who create the form in which we represent God—for our autonomy is a fiction. We are images of an Image-maker, icons of an Iconographer. We are each the action of a divine Name, the expression of its intention and its will, the form in which its action and influx are manifest. We each of us have no action but our receptivity: in so far as we receive God, God manifests Himself in us.

In the same way, every existential being is the visible form of a particular divine Name—is the being of a particular divine Name—while the divine Name constitutes the particular quality or the essential identity of the being that is its visible form. The totality of the divine Name is the Name together with the being in which it is manifest. The Name and the being in which it is manifest constitute a bi-unity, the one inseparable from the other.

Thus each created thing is also a concretization of divine Being and is embraced by this Being. All created beings possess not only Being but also the consciousness that goes with Being. Already there is life and consciousness in the most humble and elementary natural forms, however blunt and dim their revelation may be. There is always a minimum of image-quality in such forms—they are already images of Life and Reality—even though they do not reveal so well or know so well that they are such images. It is the privilege of the higher created forms—of human beings in particular—to reveal this Life and Reality more fully, and to be more conscious of their image-quality. But the ascent up the ladder of created forms from the lowest to the highest marks only a growing complexity in the formal presentation of Life and Reality, just as the descent down the ladder marks an increasing degree of concretization within divine Being. But they do not mark anything else. The difference is one of complexity and concretization, not of kind. It is a matter not of quantity but of quality. Even the lowest forms—those with the minimum degree of complexity—are already complete revelations of Life, complete revelations of divine Being. There cannot be any scission in Life and Being itself—only the material aspect of things can be multiplied by being sliced up.

The divine Names, then, achieve their meaning and full reality only through and for the beings that are their epiphanic forms—the forms in which they are manifest. This manifestation in forms is itself represented, we said, by two phases, the immaterial and the material. The immaterial phase is that through which the divine Names are individuated in forms that possess figure, pattern and body, although these lack the materiality of figures, patterns and bodies in the sensible world. These forms constitute the world of the *logoi* or Image-archetypes, the archetypes of everything that exists in the sensible world. These Image-archetypes might in their turn also be said to constitute the inner consciousness of all created beings, their inner self-awareness and identity, that which makes them what they are and nothing else. [16]

These Image-archetypes—the divine inner reality of everything—are not abstract. They are fully living, they are life itself in all its pulsating actuality and compulsion. They are the unmanifest divine Names, latent in the Father and emancipated from their unknownness in the Logos, now given vitality and beauty. If the Logos is the Image of the Father, this world of Image-archetypes is the image of this Image, its objective self-revelation or its self-determination, life-giving and life-fulfilling. In this way it is also the revelation of the Holy Spirit, for the Holy Spirit is the principle of quickening spiritual reality within the Trinity, the reality and life and beauty of the Logos of Truth.

It is the Holy Spirit that transforms the ideal, abstract Intelligence-content of the Logos into a world vibrating with the life of God: there is an Annunciation in the Trinity as well as a terrestrial Annunciation—a divine *fiat* in God Himself in relation to His own Being—and this is executed by the Holy Spirit. And it is through this Annunciation and *fiat* in God Himself that their life-giving, life-fulfilling qualities—the life of Truth in all its transparency and beauty—are bestowed on the celestial Image-archetypes, so that they, too, become the self-revelation of the Deity, the garment of God, the divine Glory that the heavens declare. [17]

Thus not only are these Image-archetypes not abstract on their own level. They are not abstract either in relation to the third phase of divine self-revelation, that which concerns the concrete realities of the visible, sensible world. Concrete existence is the living manifestation or reali-

16. For a fuller description of the idea of Image-archetypes, as of the world of the Imagination, or *mundus imaginalis*, which they constitute, see my *The Sacred in Life and Art* (Ipswich, 1990), pp.136ff.

17. Cf. Psalm 19:1.

zation of the Image-archetypes. It is not something added to them but is inherent in them. They exist concretely in things in the visible world or, rather, things in the visible world represent their temporal and spatial determinations. The invisible spiritual presence and the visible form of this presence compose an indissoluble bi-unity, with no falling away or seduction from the 'noumenal' to the 'phenomenal'. Just as the Image-archetypes are the personal living God—rooted in the personal triune Godhead—so the created world, too, is the personal living God, rooted in the same Godhead. The visible universe is the living Body of God. It is the temple of the living God.

It is at this point that we return to the theme which, as I said at the beginning of this chapter, is intimately and indissolubly wedded to the theme of creation, namely, the theme of Incarnation. For what we have been describing in these phases of divine self-revelation represents no less than the eternal process according to which the divine Logos is embodied. Assuredly, what is here in question is not so much the historical and individual Incarnation of the Logos in Jesus of Nazareth as His cosmic Incarnation. But the two are mutually supporting, and the understanding of the one illuminates the understanding of the other. In fact, one might say that the historical and individual Incarnation, and its formal interpretation, are a kind of concentrated and paradigmatic recapitulation of the cosmic Incarnation.

For what we are trying to clarify here is the theandric significance of the world, and the theandric mystery is unfolded most synoptically and unambiguously in the historical Incarnation. That is why the doctrine of creation is linked inseparably with Christology—the doctrine of the relationship of the two natures, divine and human, in Christ—and cannot properly be understood apart from Christology.

The Council of Chalcedon described the relationship between the divine and human natures in the God-man, although it did so only in negative terms: it declared that the two natures are united in Christ inseparably and unconfusedly. Created nature can never not be distinct from the divine nature, though it is important to stress that this distinction is not with respect to the source of its being but only with respect to the particular mode in which it manifests that being. This being is God's Being; and what is meant when it is said that in the God-man the divine and the human are united inseparably is that there is an interpenetration of this Being and the created element of the human. There is a symbiosis between them, even though the two partners of the union are not equal.

This, in brief, is the theandric mystery;[18] and since this mystery, consummated in Christ, is the model according to which we can understand the relationship between the divine and the human as such—for Christ's human nature is universal—and in individual human beings in particular, we can see how the potentiality in each human being for transfiguration and divinization rests upon definite and explicit ontological ground—on a potentiality intrinsic to human nature, on an inherent capacity to be divinized.

Yet this same theandric mystery is the model that applies not only with reference to our understanding of the true nature and potentiality of individual human beings; it applies also with reference to our understanding of the true nature and potentiality of each created being, down to the most humble and elementary. 'And the Logos became flesh.'[19] But 'flesh' here (*sarx*) can be taken to signify not only the flesh of the human body; it can be taken to signify all matter, all physical nature. All matter, all physical nature, is the Body of Christ.

God-manhood in its accomplishment presupposes the union of the divine and human natures in the one hypostasis of the Logos. But the interpenetration of the divine and the human in Christ corresponds precisely to the interpenetration of the particular divine Image-archetype (*logos*) and the created aspects of the natural form in which it is manifested. Christ, the divine Logos, embraces and recapitulates all the Image-archetypes of which He is the active subject and which are immanent in Him; while each creature is an individual manifestation of a single Image-archetype that, again, is immanent in its active subject, Christ. Because I am the manifestation of a divine Image-archetype in which I inhere, my true subject is Christ, for Christ is the subject of that archetype; my true self is the ego of my originating Source.

---

18. See my *The Rape of Man and Nature*, op.cit., pp.24ff. for a fuller discussion of this Christological doctrine and its anthropological implications. In effect, Christ's humanity is not something which was assumed in this world at a particular place and moment in historical time. It pertains to Him prior to all manifestation in place and time. Thus in its essence humanity is independent of spatio-temporal (and corporeal in the material sense) restrictions. And since man and God are paradigms of each other, this means that human nature is unseverably rooted in that which is uncreated and immortal. See also Meister Eckhart: 'For your human nature and that of the divine Logos are not different—it is one and the same' (from the sermon, 'Sankt Paulus spricht', in *Die Deutschen Werke*, ed. J. Quint, I. no. 24).

19. John 1:14.

The manifesting Logos includes within Himself the whole world of the Image-archetypes, and thus every created being is a manifestation of the Logos. The relationship between the Logos and His Image-archetypes (a relationship that subsumes the creaturely aspect or determination of each particular Image-archetype) constitutes the ground of the relationship between the divine and the creaturely in every created existence; and as that relationship is one of union (though not of identity), so it is also one of union (though not of identity) in every created existence. As all creation is grounded ontologically in the world of the Image-archetypes, and is their manifestation, so all creation is the Body of Christ, the Incarnation of the Logos.[20]

It is this, too, that links the doctrine of creation not only to Christology but also to the doctrine of the Trinity. In fact, it shows how all three doctrines are inextricably intertwined, and how the understanding of any one of them must be deficient unless it is set within the context of the other two. For the Image-archetypes are, as we saw, the joint revelation of the Logos and the Holy Spirit, who together disclose the unknown Father. This, we said, is because the Image-archetypes are the image of the Logos, His objective self-revelation or self-determination. Correlatively, it is the Holy Spirit who transforms the abstract, impersonal Intelligence-content of the Logos into life-giving and life-fulfilling personal forms, forms possessing a figure, a pattern, a body, irradiated with the beauty of God. One could say that the Image-archetypes that are the self-expression of the Logos are given birth through the agency of the Holy Spirit.

Thus the Image-archetypes disclose both the Logos and the Holy Spirit together and simultaneously. Yet since the created dimension of each Image-archetype is subsumed within the Image-archetype itself, this dimension, too, discloses both Persons together: it is an example of God-creaturehood in exactly the same way as Christ is the prototype of God-manhood. It, too, and all creation with it, is an unfolding of the theandric mystery. It, too, and all creation with it, is a disclosure of divine personality.

This is to say that the Image-archetypes, together with their spatio-temporal endorsement, are themselves types of divine manhood, or

20. See St Maximos the Confessor and reference given in note 14 above. A *locus classicus* in this respect in St Maximos's writings is to be found in P.G. 91, 1329 ABC. See also Ruysbroeck, *The Adornment of the Spiritual Marriage*, trs. C.A. Wynschenk Dom (London, 1951), pp.172–73.

divine creaturehood. That is why just as is the case for individual human beings, so for each created form in the natural world its potentiality for transfiguration and divinization rests upon definite and explicit ontological ground—on a potentiality intrinsic to it, on an inherent capacity to be divinized. And it is upon exactly this same ground that is based the reality of the promise that 'God may be all in all'[21]—the promise that God may become all in all *within* the creaturely existence of this universe.

We are now in a position to see more clearly the significance of what I emphasized briefly above, namely that the generation of the Logos, the Son and Image of the Father, is linked inseparably to the cosmogonic act, the act of creation. We have seen how the Logos as abstract and impersonal Intelligence-content is given living and personal form through the Holy Spirit in the still immaterial Image-archetypes. This means that on the one side there is potential Sonship—the unexpressed, impersonal Logos-Intelligence—while on the other side there are the forms in which personal Sonship is actually realized, the forms of the living Image-archetypes, though these two phases or 'moments' in the generation of the Son are simultaneous, take place in instantaneity.

There is thus generation of the Son prior to creation. But since the single simple act of this generation of the Son includes the generation of that aspect of Sonship which is given character and personality in the world of the Image-archetypes, it follows that this act of generation includes within it and finds its full expression in the act of creation, in and through the manifestation of the forms of the created world. For all the concrete, visible forms of created things are subsumed in the Image-archetypes, are but their spatio-temporal effects, or prolongations, or counterparts.

Thus the generation of the Son is at once both generation prior to creation and simultaneously generation in creation. Generation and creation are linked inseparably: they are distinct yet inseparable 'moments', or aspects, of a single creative act, and there can be no Sonship without simultaneously the unfolding of the living forms of created existence.

Indeed, the Logos as the full Image of the Father is not the Logos only in so far as He discloses the unmanifest potentialities of the Divine in an ideal, abstract sense; the full Image is the Logos in so far as He also manifests these potentialities in both the immaterial forms of the

21. I Cor. 15:28.

Image-archetypes and in the forms of their spatial and temporal realization in the material world. He is, that is to say, the full Image in so far as He is not only the Son of God but is also the Son of Man. And the fact that these two 'moments' in His generation are distinct indicates the distinction between divine Sonship and temporal and spatial creatureliness, as well as to how the second depends on the first and not *vice versa*; while the fact that they are inseparable again testifies to the accomplishment of the theandric mystery whereby the natural forms of this world are each and all incarnations of the divine Logos.

It might be assumed that here we can call a halt, and that the thesis which we set out to establish—how and why created realities are sacred—has been established. Unfortunately, this is not the case—or at least not the case unless we choose to pass over in silence two major questions that not only are extremely intractable in themselves but also may be said to posit the ultimate paradoxes of human thought. Not to speak of them, therefore, however inadequately, would be to jeopardize the credibility of all that has been said in this chapter, since what has been said appears to ignore these two crucial and absolutely fundamental questions.

The first question concerns, quite simply, the problem of evil. All I have said so far in this chapter, and some of the things I shall say in the remaining pages, presuppose that things are in their natural state, the state in which they ought to be, and that we see them as we ought to see them. But it is quite clear—and the main thrust of some of the earlier chapters in this book has been directed to emphasizing this—that a great deal of what confronts us in our world is far from natural, and that we are only too prone to see things in a way that represents a complete distortion of their reality, a complete violation of their true being. In fact, we can only see things as they are when we see them with the same eyes as those with which God sees them. This means that when we fail—as for the most part we do fail—to see them in this way, then we see them only according to the mode in which our own sight, restricted, coloured and even blinded by ignorance and prejudice, permits us to see them. Thus inevitably, to a greater or lesser degree, we fail both to see things as they are in reality, and to treat them accordingly.

Again, it may be perfectly true, as we said above, that each thing possesses the capacity to move from an imperfect harmony with God (and hence with itself) to a perfect harmony, the perfect harmony being achieved when the personal *logos* and *sophia* of each created being is the effective and determinative subject of that being. But it is quite clear—and again the main thrust of some of the earlier chapters is directed to emphasizing this—that this capacity is all too seldom exercised, let alone brought to fruition, and that what confronts us in our world is only too often evidence of total disharmony, whether between man and God or between man and other forms of created being. Just as the divine image in us must be our organ of perception if we are to see things as God sees them—for then our soul becomes God's organ of perception—so it is the divine image in us, as in all other things, that alone is capable of accomplishing the movement from imperfection to perfection through which our self-sundered, vitiated and often vicious state is overcome. And the truth is that the way we see things, and the actual state in which for the most part we live, testify not so much to our desire to nourish and affirm the divine image in us as to our abject failure to do so.

In other words, we are under the influence of a power of negation that induces us to think and act in ways that, far from being in accord with, are contrary to and destructive of the natural order of things; and it is this power that we designate as evil. It is here that the paradox of which I spoke presents itself. For nothing that exists can be bad, since all that exists, and existence itself, derive from and are rooted in God, in whom there is no evil whatsoever. Hence all things are good in so far as they exist. Correspondingly, there can be nothing that is totally evil, for—since everything that exists is good—to be totally evil would be to be non-existent.

Evil in itself, therefore, can have no existence. As Julian of Norwich confirms, 'it has no substance or real existence.'[22] And St Maximos the Confessor is even more emphatic:

As a reality in itself evil never has been and never will be in existence; for it does not in any way whatsoever possess being, or reality, or substance, or power, or activity among existent things. It is neither a quantity, nor a quality, nor a relationship, nor a place, nor time, nor position. It is not a making, or an activity, or a habitude, or a passion, such as may naturally characterize certain beings, and nor has it acquired any existence in its own right in any of these things.[23]

22. Julian of Norwich, *Revelations of Divine Love*, xxvii.
23. St Maximos the Confessor, *Quaest. ad Thalassium*, P.G. 90, 253 B. See also St Dionysios the Areopagite, who in his *The Divine Names* (iv. 32) describes evil as

Here, then, we are at once confronted with the paradox in question. For though evil possesses no metaphysical reality, yet on all sides in the world in which we actually live there is more than enough evidence for our endless complicity in and contribution to ways of thought and action, public and private, that are as depraving as they are depraved. Whatever the original and intrinsic nature of things, our actual finite world is literally soaked in evil; and it would be as self-delusive as it is self-evasive for us to pretend that these facts of evil are not facts of evil.

So we are faced with the enigma of how, in a world in which by definition everything that exists is good, evil has as much reality as the good. We are faced with the enigma of why men in the mass, far from moving from imperfection to perfection, appear infinitely to prefer the anonymity of their non-being to affirming and revealing the Name that aspires to find in their love and nobility the epiphany of its own being. One may say that this evil is but an apparent reality; yet in one sense our whole finite world is but an apparent reality, though it is not on that account any the less real for us who live in it and who suffer from the evil rampant in it. Or we can say that evil is but a lapse and failure on our part, and so is merely negative; yet this lapse and failure have about them something unequivocally positive—just as positive as the values and virtues from which we lapse. The reality presented by the absence or denial of qualities that are life-giving and life-enhancing consists precisely in the void which that absence or denial creates, a void necessarily life-sapping and even life-destructive.

For in the same passage as that in which St Maximos affirms the ultimate unreality of evil, he also describes evil as a defect in the energy capable of bringing about the fulfilment of the natural powers and possibilities inherent in created beings. It is, he says, a deviation, produced by an act of mistaken judgment, of these natural powers away from the goal or purpose in which their fruition resides towards ends that debase and degrade the being concerned, making it abandon its proper rank in the order of creation in order to usurp an inferior rank. This usurpation in its turn does violence not only to the being in question but also to the whole harmony of things as such.

It is essentially in such an act of self-degradation leading to the abuse of

---

'unfounded, uncaused, indeterminate, unborn, inert, powerless, disordered. It is errant, indefinite, dark, insubstantial, never in itself possessed of any existence') (Luibheid's trs. in *Pseudo-Dionysius: The Complete Works*, op. cit.).

other created realities that evil is manifest. In our natural state—the state in which we are originally created and which remains a potentiality of our being however much we may be unaware of it or fail to recognize it—we see and know ourself as part of a universe made by God. We know ourself called upon to fill our place in the universal order, to which we must submit ourself by referring ourself and all things to which we are related to that common end or source in which alone we, together with all other things, can fulfil the capacities inherent in our nature. It is only thus that we can realize the harmony that is the law of our being because it is intrinsic to the Being from whom we derive and by participation in whom we alone possess life and reality.

If, on the other hand, we refuse to accept this order and, instead of referring ourself and all things to which we are related to our common source, refer everything to ourself, we commit an act of apostasy, a denial of God, which inevitably results in that act of self-degradation and abuse of other created realities of which I have spoken. Our thought is then preoccupied with things in order to use them to serve our own purposes, regarding them as objects in their own right which we are entitled to exploit as such. It is in this movement of thought that consists essentially the avarice which is said to be the root of evil.[24]

Such avarice is a disposition of our soul which refuses to acknowledge and share in the destiny common to all things and which desires to possess and use all things for itself, as if these things existed only to satisfy our own individual or mass cupidity. Realizing our power over things, we become so addicted to this domination that we proclaim it to be our natural right; and we become impervious to the fact that through this seeming act of self-aggrandizement we actually debase the whole of our existence, perverting and even destroying the natural harmony of our being as well as that of everything with which we come into contact.

Such a movement of thought has its origin, according to St Maximos, in an act of mistaken judgment. But an act of mistaken judgment on the part of a human being is possible only on condition that human beings are created with the capacity to exercise a freedom of choice; for only through such freedom could we possess the liberty to choose evil. This means that our capacity for evil is inherent in our capacity for self-determination: we possess the capacity to deny the reality of our own being or to affirm it and to act in accordance with it; we possess the

24. See I Tim. 6:10.

capacity to deny the reality of other created beings or to affirm it and to act in accordance with it. As St Simeon the New Theologian states: 'None of us can be estranged or alienated from the nature in which we are created. We are created good by God—for God creates nothing evil—and we remain unchanging in our nature and essence as created. But we do what we choose and want, whether good or bad, of our own free will.'[25]

The enigma of evil is, therefore, rooted in the ultimate mystery of our creation in the image of God as spiritual beings unbound by any necessity or external constraint, and capable of maintaining our identity as the image of God unconditioned by any such constraint through fusing our being with that of our divine archetype. We are created free in God, not in our own selfhood; and any exercise of this freedom that involves the assertion of our selfhood as a reality essentially other than and independent of the divine archetype inevitably results in a loss of identity that is tantamount to that act of self-degradation and self-destruction in which evil is manifest. What we call evil is, then, a tendency in us to destroy ourselves. Ultimately it is a tendency towards spiritual death.

We can now see why the act of mistaken judgment in which lies, according to St Maximos, the origin of evil, may also represent a mistaken quest for the good. For a condition of maintaining our identity as the image of God as an actuality and not simply as a potentiality, is precisely that we refuse to assert our individual selfhood as a reality essentially other than and independent of our divine archetype. It is that we make a continuous act of self-negation through which we acknowledge that the core of our being resides not in our own selfhood but in God.

Yet evil, too, involves an act of self-negation and even of self-extinction. Now, however, this act does not consist in affirming that the true centre of our humanity resides in God and not in our own selfhood or ego. On the contrary, it consists in our asserting the substantial independence of our ego and thereby setting out on a course of self-destruction that ends up, or may end up, in the negation of our reality as human beings, a negation that involves the negation of the reality of everything else as well. The mistaken judgment is to identify ourself not with that which confirms the union of the human with the divine and the divine with the human, but

25. St Simeon the New Theologian, *Practical and Theological Texts*, in *Philokalia*, vol. 3 (Athens, 1960), text 110, p.258.

with that which, at least in thought, sets them apart and which manifests itself as our gravitation towards self-extinction and non-existence.

For if evil is ultimately non-existent, it must manifest itself on the existential plane in terms of non-existence in the sense that it induces in those it qualifies a movement of thought and action away from existence towards non-existence (which is itself a non-existent category), away from reality towards annihilation and spiritual death. This in its turn means—and here the paradox again asserts itself—that things are non-existent in so far as they are evil. It also means that it is only through battening vampire-like on what exists that evil can manifest itself at all; and since by definition all that exists is good, this is tantamount to saying that without the good evil can get no purchase. The ugliness of evil consists in the corruption of something that is essentially good. It is only because we are essentially good that we have the capacity for evil. It is only because we are potentially divine that we can be satanic. And a corollary that depends from this is that if we are not essentially good and potentially divine, then nothing we do, however bestial, despicable and inhuman it may appear, is in the end actually either evil or satanic.

This capacity for evil, which we possess by virtue of the fact that as the image of God we also possess the capacity for self-determination, is set in motion when we invest with reality, or give positive value to, some image or thought that is essentially illusory and then proceed to act in accordance with it and to implement it in terms of our practical living. It is linked, therefore, decisively to our capacity for self-delusion—for mistaking our identity—and the multiple forms this may take. It is also a corollary to this that each step we make into the world of illusion—which is also the world of self-deception—leads us ever further from self-knowledge and our true identity, and plunges us ever more deeply into the world of ignorance and self-forgetfulness.

It is because of this chain of consequences set in motion by every act of mistaken judgment that over the generations individual men and women, and whole collectivities of men and women, may become so enmeshed in thought-forms and practices of evil, and hence so self-blinded and self-alienated, that they call down on themselves their own nemesis together with that of the world they inhabit. It is hardly necessary to say that such a state of self-blindness and self-alienation characterizes the dominant social collectivities in the contemporary world.

Yet at the same time it must be reaffirmed that human beings, whether severally or collectively, cannot ultimately extinguish their own existence. Neither they, nor even the demons, can ultimately destroy the image of the Godhead within them, however much they may defile and foul it. This means that however far along the path of self-deception we may have advanced, we can never ultimately lose the capacity to make and implement a decision that represents, even if initially but to a fractional degree, a movement away from this path and towards the recovery of our true being and reality, as well as the awareness of those of every other created thing. And such an act may have incalculable consequences not only for the individual who makes it but also for the collectivity of which he is a member and for the life of the world about him. And in this connection we must always remember, first, that in its essence everything is incorruptible, immortal and timeless, and that God can never cease from being the Creator of a creation which at each instant is reborn *from the beginning* in all its pristine innocence and beauty; and, second, that if we do not know what we are in our natural state, we will not realize to what, through our connivance in evil, we have debased ourselves.

That is why it is so important for us to reaffirm the true reality of things, including ourselves, in their natural state; for this state is not simply that in which things ought to be, it is also that in which they actually are if only we could see them aright. Unless we become conscious of our inherent nobility, as well as that of every other existing thing, we are not likely to be stirred to make even the slightest gesture capable of initiating a movement of thought and action towards the recovery of our lost spiritual vision and being. And this is equivalent to saying that we are not likely to be stirred to make such a gesture while we are still victims of the kind of fraudulent self-image and world-view that has dominated our thought and action over the last few centuries and that still continues to dominate them.[26]

26. These few remarks about evil do not pretend to provide anything like a definitive answer to the problem of evil. At best they but indicate the kind of coordinates that have to be taken into account if we are not radically to misapprehend its essentially paradoxical character. Above all, I hope that at least they make it clear that any attempt to 'resolve' this paradox, either by attributing to evil an ontological reality which it could possess only on condition that it is rooted in God, or by deducing from the fact of its ultimate metaphysical non-existence the conclusion that its manifestation on the existential plane is characterized by a similar unreality, represents an aberration that confuses the issue in the worst possible way. For to say that the source of evil lies in God Himself is to assert that it is also endemic to human beings as such, since human beings are created in the image of God; and this is both to absolve human beings from responsibility for its manifestation on the existential

The second question that must be addressed, if the credibility of the main thesis of this chapter is not to be jeopardized, relates to a problem I touched on when speaking above about pantheism. We must now confront this problem more fully and openly for, as we shall see, its confrontation brings into the centre of the cosmological scheme I have been trying to delineate a figure that so far has received no direct mention and that yet is crucial to its whole integrity.

Let us first restate the problem. What I have been outlining in this chapter is a doctrine of creation that closes the door—or is meant to close the door—on the kind of dualism which, we said, has for various reasons crept into Christian theology. This dualism takes the form of positing creation as something exterior to God. It is a concept that is rooted in an unrelenting pluralism; and even if in the final analysis this pluralism is reduced to two, God and creature, beyond that it cannot be reduced: there is no divinization of the creature. It is a concept that either tends to result in turning God into an autarchic, transcendent tyrant who has His terrestrial counterpart in a religio-socio collectivity that seeks to impose a totalitarian monotheism upon everyone; or it tends to degenerate into the idolatry that sees creation as a separate existence outside God and ultimately leads to the desecration of things so typical of our own times.

As against this concept I have been positing the idea of a creation that exists within God, that is rooted in God, and of which God is the single ultimate subject. But if we insist that God is the sole ultimate subject of creation, how can we not end up in some form of Monism which annihilates men and creatures before and into the divine Uniqueness? Or, alternatively, if the absoluteness of the Absolute is combined with

---

plane, and correspondingly to deny that human beings possess that capacity for self-determination which in fact constitutes the bedrock of their true dignity. It is also to deny that intrinsic to creation is the possibility of existing in a state that is free from evil, a possibility of which in the Christian tradition we are given the gage both in the typology of paradise (a created reality which prior to the 'fall' is free from any admixture of evil), and in the fact that Christ's created nature is said to be free of sin. To maintain, on the other hand, that because evil possesses no metaphysical reality its appearance on the existential plane must be characterized by a similar unreality, is to try to evade and minimize in the most callous kind of way its only too real actuality and the only too real suffering it produces in every form of created existence. It is also most subtly to condone, and hence to connive in, those very acts of brutality and desecration through which we give it this actuality in our criminal attempts to assert our dominion over both other human beings and the world of nature. For of what are we guilty if all this is basically unreal?

the relationship that links each creature to God—if the divine life is joined to its manifestation in the created universe—how is the transcendent and undifferentiated Oneness of the Absolute not totally disrupted? In trying to avoid a dualism we seem, then, either to be in danger of falling victim to a Monism that promotes an acosmism or anti-cosmism which reduces the world and particular beings to unaccountable appearances or even illusions, and easily degenerates into the anti-aesthetic pseudo-asceticism of which I have spoken; or to be in danger of splintering the simplicity and transcendence of the Absolute into limitless polytheism.

The problem, then, is how to differentiate in the Absolute One without disrupting its oneness or depriving the many creatures *qua* creatures of eternal and sacred value; and this I have attempted to do in the cosmology I have been describing. But if in so doing I may have avoided the pitfall of dualism, is it clear how God can be all in all within the creaturely existence of this universe unless we either admit an extreme form of pantheism which annihilates the reality of the creature as such, or confess that His absolute oneness is shattered and His transcendence eclipsed by His immanence?

For if God Himself, whether as the hypostasis of the Logos or as any Person of the Trinity, mediates Himself in His Absolute Being directly to creation, then one of these two consequences must follow—must follow unless we acknowledge that in creating the world God creates it outside Himself, in which case we again fall into the dualism we are trying to avoid. For if God both creates the world within Himself—from His own Being—and mediates Himself in His Absolute Being directly to the world, there can be no possible distinction of any kind between the two: God and the world must form a single absolute identity.

Thus God cannot mediate Himself directly in this manner. Yet so far, although I have spoken of a world—the world of the divine Image-archetypes—that is intermediate between the transcendent Deity and the visible world, I have said nothing at all of any principle in the Divine that is other than God whereby God mediates Himself to the world in a way that preserves both His transcendence and the full significance of the world as the Body of God, as the accomplishment of the theandric mystery. It is this principle that we must now try to identify.

In fact, the task may not be so difficult, especially if we recall the observation I made above to the effect that the living Image-archetypes constitute the self expression of the divine Logos and that they are given

175

birth through the agency of the Holy Spirit. It is through this act that God acquires His Lordship and thus properly speaking becomes God. God cannot be God to or in Himself—in Himself He is simply what He is. He can be God only to those to whom He gives being, to those other beings in relationship to whom He has the status of Godhood.[27] It is the birth of God in the Image-archetypes that establishes this relationship. One might say that it is through the birth of the Image-archetypes that God Himself is given birth; for through that birth He gives being to those over whom He is Lord and so to those in relationship to whom He is God. The birth in God of the Image-archetypes constitutes an act of interior hierarchization within the Divine, the interior founding of a subordinate rank.

This is why I said it may not be so difficult to identify the mediating principle that we seek. For to give birth is a maternal function. The act of self-expression in God—the act through which the subordinate rank within God is founded—demands therefore the recognition of a feminine principle in the Divine, as the medium by means of which, and as the *locus* within which, the Image-archetypes—God's revelations of His totally unknown and unmanifest Being—are given birth. The feminine principle in the Divine is the receptacle in which the Image-archetypes, formless and abstract in the Intelligence-content of the Logos, are given figure, pattern and body, albeit still immaterial—figure, pattern and body filled with the reality and beauty of the Holy Spirit, life-giving and life-fulfilling. The essence of the Feminine in the Divine is to disclose in the transparency and beauty of living forms the Being by whom she herself is disclosed. In this way she establishes that relationship by virtue of which God becomes God. In this way she gives birth to God.

This is the secret of the term, Mother of God (Theotokos), as it is also the secret of the initial cosmogonic act. The Mother of God is the Virgin Mother or the unconditioned holy Wisdom—*Sophia aeterna*—through whom God reveals Himself to Himself by manifesting the virtualities of His divine Names, the prototypes of all created being latent in His unknown and transcendent Being. It is the revelation by means of which God acquires His Godhood.

27. See Meister Eckhart's statement, 'If I were not, God would not be God', in his sermon 52, 'Beati Pauperes spiritu'. See also Angelus Silesius, 'I know that without me, the life of God were lost', and 'God is nothing at all, and if He is something, only in me it is' (*The Cherubic Wanderer*, 1, 8 and 1,200, trs. Willard R. Trask, New York, 1953).

In this respect the Mother of God is a passive potency, the 'immaterial matter' in whom the Image-archetypes 'take flesh', or 'take body', though not initially a material, physical body. She is the universal spiritual substance, the universal Nature—*Natura naturans*—in which flower all the forms of being—everything that is differentiated from God's Being as such—from the highest archangels down to the most elementary material organisms. She is herself the embracing organism of the pre-existent forms of all that visibly comes into existence. She is the divine ground in which all things lie from eternity, the mirror in which God beholds Himself: 'For she is the brightness of eternal light, and the unspotted mirror of God's life.'[28] It is not for nothing that she is celebrated as 'more honourable than the cherubim, incomparably more glorious than the seraphim' and is greeted as the 'Unwedded Bride', the 'illumination of those initiated into the mysteries of the Holy Trinity'.[29]

To speak of the divine feminine principle in this way may give the impression that I am simply substituting one form of dualism for another; that instead of a dualism between God and creation I am now positing a dualism between God and this feminine principle, as if it was a fourth hypostasis or Person independent of the other three. This is not the case at all. It is true that the divine Feminine—this holy Wisdom—though situated in God and other than God, is yet an 'other' that possesses full ontological reality; but this does not mean she is a fourth hypostasis or is a reality in God that is independent of the three Persons of the Trinity.

28. Wisdom of Solomon 7:26. For other characterizations of Sophia in Old Testament literature, see Wisdom of Solomon 7:7–14, 22–30; 8:1ff.; 9:9–11; 10:1ff.; Proverbs 8:22–30; Ecclesiasticus 7:1–20; 4:11–19.

29. *The Akathistos Hymn*. Many of the characterizations of the Mother of God in this Hymn are either unintelligible or so hyperbolic as to be absurd unless they are understood to refer to her transhistorical and universal role as a cosmic principle—her role as Sophia aeterna, the Eternal Feminine. The same applies to many of her characterizations in Orthodox Christian homilies and liturgical texts: see in this respect the examples cited by Mary Cunningham in her article, 'The Mother of God in early Byzantine Homilies' (*Sobornost*, 10:2, 1988, pp.53–67). For the recognition of a similar role attributed to the Mother of God in the Syriac theological tradition, see the articles of Sebastian Brock, 'World and Sacrament in the Writings of the Syrian Fathers', 'The Mysteries hidden in the side of Christ', 'Mary and the Eucharist' (in *Sobornost*, 6:10, 1974, pp. 685–98; 7:6, 1978, pp.462–77; 1:2, 1979, pp.50–59 respectively), and 'Mary in Syriac Tradition' (Ecumenical Society of the Blessed Virgin, London, 1977), as well as R. Murray, 'Mary the Second Eve in the early Syriac Fathers' (ECR 3, 1971, pp.372–84).

Wisdom is not and cannot be a self-supporting existence; she does not in any way split God into two Beings, or multiply reality into two. She exists for God and in God, is rooted in God. In so far as God and His Wisdom are two, they are two that compose one, just as mother and unborn child are one, or man and woman are one in the nuptial union, or the two natures in the God-man are one, inseparably yet without confusion. They constitute an identity-in-distinction, an indissoluble bi-unity.

From another angle one could say that God and His Wisdom are two that compose one just as the Trinity is three that compose One. But here the analogy in one important respect does not hold good. For while in the Trinity the three Persons are of equal rank, in the God-Wisdom bi-unity there is not this equality. God and His Wisdom are linked together in their very being, 'either is the other's mine', they are indissoluble, neither can exist apart from their connection with each other, they need each other not only to be but also to be more fully, in order that the essential nature of each of them is expressed more fully. But in spite of this they are not equal partners. They embrace each other in a relationship of subordination or hierarchy.

For God never has His reality in a being other than His own. Wisdom has her being in God's Being. She is the counterpart of God, but she is not God. Though she is God's Mother and His Glory, she is yet other than God. There is both unity and 'otherness' in the relationship between them, a unity and 'otherness' reflected in the relationship between the creature and its Creator. Wisdom in the God-Wisdom bi-unity is always the lower unit, just as the pattern-qualities in visible phenomena are always their lower unit. She is eternally immanent in God, God is never without her, yet in His absoluteness God infinitely transcends her.

Yet it should here be emphasized that from another and more profound point of view this relationship of subordination and hierarchy between God and the feminine principle in the Divinity is reversed, and it is the feminine principle that is the higher unit. We have seen that the Mother of God is as it were the womb in which the Image-archetypes are conceived and that in this respect she is the universal Nature in which the Father eternally begets the manifested Son, the divine Logos. But in so far as the Father, the supreme masculine principle, as the power that makes things be, may be distinguished from the divine Mother, the Magna Mater, as the power that enables them to be, so the role that the latter plays *in divinis* may be seen to be superlatively operative in a prior phase of the process in which God reveals Himself to Himself. For here the Feminine is the pure potentiality that transcends even Being or Essence itself: she is 'beyond Being', 'that which is not', the *Nihil* or totally occluded state that is a precondition of God being able to be at all, or to know and affirm Himself at all. As such she is the principle of the masculine principle itself, as that which makes it possible for God to constitute and to deploy His very divinity.

Of course, as already stressed, the presence of a masculine and a feminine principle *in divinis* does not mean that there is a dualism in the Supreme Reality, for the two are one, constituting a divine bi-unity and conjunction of Essence and Nature. But it does mean that the Supreme Reality can be designated either as Masculine or as Feminine, or as both simultaneously; and it also means that while in relation to the manifested Son, and hence is relation to creation as a whole, it may be said that the Feminine is subordinate to the Masculine, in relation to the ultimate mysteries of the Godhead it may be said that the Masculine is subordinate to the Feminine: in that realm the Feminine is in an ultimate sense the Mother of God.

The divine Feminine is, then, the *locus* or receptacle in which God begets the Divine Names—the virtualities of His Being—in living individuated forms. But she is not simply a passive potency. She does not give birth only to the spiritual dimension of created existence. She has an active cosmological role. For in her—in her all-embracing unity—is contained the fulness of the world of the Image-archetypes. Yet, as we remarked, these Image-archetypes are not abstract in relation to the concrete realities of the visible world. On the contrary, concrete sensible realities are the living manifestation or realization of the Image-archetypes. They are not something added to them. They inhere in them, are immanent in them. They represent their temporal and spatial expression and determination. Thus, since this virginal figure of holy Wisdom contains within herself the world of Image-archetypes, she also contains within herself the created aspect or dimension that inheres within them: she embraces the two aspects, uncreated and created, invisible and visible, of their indissoluble bi-unity.

It is in this respect that the divine Feminine also possesses an active potency. She is the principle that receives substantive Being and Life, but she is also the principle that informs them, shows them forth in forms, manifests them in forms. She does not constitute Being or Life, but she transposes them. God makes things to be, gives them life and reality; Wisdom gives them a form, a figure, a body. She is not herself the active

179

principle of creation, but she presides over the creative process. She is the artificer of all things—*i ton panton teknitis*—present with God when He makes the world,[30] and His companion in giving things their harmony and fitness;[31] but she does not herself create. She is needed to mediate between the potential and the actual, to differentiate between the potential and the actual, and to radiate God's reality and life in the finite world; but she is not the source of this reality and life.

Yet without the instrumentality of her motherhood God's self-revelation in the world of created beings could never occur; for it is from her more than angelic nature that created beings take the pattern-qualities which characterize the shifting, manifest forms of this world.

Yet what she manifests is never itself merely patternness, never mere appearance. Created beings are infinitely more than anything that can be expressed in mathematical terms, for what their visible forms enshrine is the divine life in all its fulness. This life is not impaired or reduced by the form-limit that it receives. Its glory and full radiance may be folded up or pleated, but they are not depleted or lost. They are fully present. The limitation or conditioned state into which God brings Himself in creation has nothing to do with Being as such, it concerns only the mode in which Being is manifest. Being itself is one and indivisible, and remains one and indivisible no matter how many forms it may be present in. There is no pantheism, but there is what might be called panentheism, which is quite a different matter.

This is why the beauty and love with which the Holy Spirit quickens the celestial Image-archetypes are not different from but are identical with the beauty and love with which He quickens their created counterparts. This, too, is why sensible beauty—beauty in all natural forms—is so much more than simply an aesthetic quality, is why it possesses an intrinsic spiritual potency. For it is the similitude—the signature—of the divine Beauty that God contemplates from all eternity.[32] And just as it is divine Beauty that sets in motion the movement whereby God reveals His potentiality in manifest forms, so it is the same beauty revealed in these same forms that rouses in individual created beings the aspiration for higher existence that is present potentially in all of them. And just as it is God's love for the world

30. *Wisdom of Solomon* 7:21 and 9:9.

31. Proverbs 8:30.

32. Cf. St Gregory of Nazianzos, Carm. theol. IV. De Mundo, V, 67–68. P.G. 36, 421).

that brings God to birth in manhood—that accomplishes the theandric mystery in all things—so it is this same love that fills all creatures with the aspiration for perfect love. In both cases the aspiration in created beings is itself a divine aspiration.

The theandric mystery—the mystery of God-manhood, of the Incarnate Logos—is, then, that through which the sacramental reality of the created world is consummated. And the being through whom it is consummated is the Mother of God, whether in her universal plenitude as divine Wisdom or as the individualization of this Wisdom in the person of the All-Holy Virgin Mary. For what is created is contained in and is one with its uncreated prototype, and both together represent the fulness of the Image-archetypes embraced by eternal Wisdom and constituting her reality. The divine world of Wisdom is the prototype of the created world; but the created world is itself this same Wisdom in her created aspect. Although she is one, she exists in two modes, eternal and temporal, uncreated and created.

Thus the Mother of God is not simply the foundation of the world of creatures: she is herself this world. While remaining always spiritual, above space and time, she is also the root of what is material, spatial and temporal. She is not only *Natura naturans*, she is also *Natura naturata*. She is Earth as a single immaterial feminine divinity, and she is earth as a manifold, material reality. She is herself the Body of the cosmic Christ, the created matrix in whom the divine Logos eternally takes flesh. She is the bridge that unites God to the world, the world to God, and it is she that bestows on the world its eternal and sacred value. She is the seal of its sacred identity.

Index

183

BY THE SAME AUTHOR

Orientation and Descent (poems)
The Marble Threshing Floor: Studies in Modern Greek Poetry
The Greek East and the Latin West
Athos: The Mountain of Silence
Six Poets of Modern Greece (with Edmund Keeley)
Constantinople: The Iconography of a Sacred City
The Pursuit of Greece (editor)
Byzantium
George Seferis: Collected poems (1924–1955) (with Edmund Keeley)
Modern Greece (with John Campbell)
C. P. Cavafy: Selected Poems (with Edmund Keeley)
W. B. Yeats and the Search for Tradition (essay)
C. P. Cavafy: Collected Poems (with Edmund Keeley)
Christianity and Eros: Essays on the Theme of Sexual Love
Church, Papacy, and Schism: A Theological Enquiry
The Wound of Greece: Studies in Neo-Hellenism
The Philokalia (with G. E. H. Palmer and Kallistos Ware)
Motets for a Sunflower (poems)
Angelos Sikelianos: Selected Poems (with Edmund Keeley)
Odysseus Elytis: Selected Poems (with Edmund Keeley)
*The Rape of Man and Nature: An Enquiry into the Origins and Consequences
    of Modern Science*
The Sacred in Life and Art
Edward Lear: The Corfu Years (editor)
In the Sign of the Rainbow: Selected Poems 1940–1989
George Seferis: Complete Poems (with Edmund Keeley)
For Every Thing That Lives is Holy (essay)
Christianity: Lineaments of a Sacred Tradition